/18

such a blessing to our family.
I pray this book will be a blessing to you!

THE INSIDE-OUT CHURCH

Dennis Lanning

My first book

DENNIS LANNING

THE
INSIDE-OUT
CHURCH

TATE PUBLISHING
AND ENTERPRISES, LLC

Published by Tate Publishing & Enterprises, LLC
127 E. Trade Center Terrace | Mustang, Oklahoma 73064 USA
1.888.361.9473 | www.tatepublishing.com

Tate Publishing is committed to excellence in the publishing industry. The company reflects the philosophy established by the founders, based on Psalm 68:11,
"The Lord gave the word and great was the company of those who published it."

Published in the United States of America

ISBN: 978-1-63063-822-1
1. Religion / Christian Church / Growth
2. Religion / Christian Life / General
14.02.20

DEDICATION

To the Sunday evening congregation of
Avalon United Methodist Church

ACKNOWLEDGMENTS

I would like to thank the congregation of Avalon United Methodist Church, where I serve as pastor, for their unwavering encouragement of this project. It started as an ongoing story of which I would share a chapter each Sunday night at worship. The congregation listened to the story with great interest and always seemed eager to hear the next chapter.

My wife, Joy, continues to be my biggest fan. There is no one God could have brought my way that would be a better match for my needs.

I am amazed at the skill and insights of Pat Jones, who carefully read through and corrected my manuscript. I applaud you and thank you!

The people at Tate Publishing have been a pleasure to work with. They make a writer feel cared for and accepted as part of the family. Bravo!

PREFACE

The religious landscape is changing. Many historic churches find their average attendance dropping each year. New churches seem to get bigger, while the established churches seem unable to find the key to growth. The small church, especially, struggles to attract enough people to keep basic programs viable.

Most churches consider themselves friendly and rightfully so. We have more churches than ever before that have a system in place which intends to make visitors feel valued. Visiting families are treated very well.

The problem is not how we treat people that come to us. Christianity has lost much of its outward focus. We no longer know how to go into our communities and invite people to attend our houses of worship.

I really don't think inviting people to meet Christ and church members is an impossible task. For the most part, we just need to turn our lives inside out. We must decide that we will think of others first.

What would a church look like if it decided to live inside out?

CHAPTER 1

The honeymoon was over.

Tom Osborn took over as pastor of Old Dominion United Methodist Church last June. Attendance increased for awhile, but now the excitement a new spiritual leader brings was waning. After seven months, this church was slipping into habits, and not every habit was good.

He stood up from his desk and looked slowly around the office. Striding to the lone bookshelf, he took all the books on preaching he owned and stacked them in the middle of the floor. Soon a stack related to evangelism stood next to it, then theology, leadership, and counseling.

When all six shelves were empty, the pastor slid the bookshelf six feet to the right, and pulled his oak desk into the vacated space.

Thirty minutes later, every piece of furniture in the office had found a new home.

Change was good. It was time for a revival. Tom was determined it would start with him.

"It's so easy for a Christian to turn his or her focus inward, on themselves," Reverend Springstead said.

He paused and let his brown eyes roam from person to person in the Sunday night congregation of Old Dominion United Methodist Church.

It was the first night of revival services, the first this church had had in several years.

The guest evangelist resumed his sermon. "People mainly think of themselves. Isn't that true? And you need not think you're the only one. Throughout the Bible, we see the same thing happen to humanity over and over. It was evident on the day the devil told Adam and Eve, 'You can be like God,' and they chose their own way; and that time King David saw Bathsheba from his rooftop and took her for himself; and when Pharisee Saul made a name for himself by jailing Jesus's followers. From the beginning, we have had the tendency to turn our attention to the mirror, to gaze upon ourselves."

The lanky sixty-year-old stepped from behind the pulpit and began to walk down to the front of the center aisle. "It happens to me, and I know that I'm not unique. There are days when I ponder what *I* have done for God, what *I* have accomplished. I think about *my* plans for the future. Friends, I forget that there are a whole lot of other people on this planet, and God loves them all as much as he does me."

William Springstead was now at floor level. "God wants every person to be saved. We read that in First Timothy. God wants everybody to come to the knowledge of truth, and Jesus said you shall know the truth, and the truth shall set you free. So if you and I are thinking mainly about ourselves, how are the people who have no relationship with God ever going to hear the good news? How are they going to find out that there is so much more than these seventy or so years we live in this body? How will they hear about eternity? How will they find the fulfilling life we know? How will they know that Jesus died on the cross to open the door to all this?"

Reverend Springstead let that last thought linger in the air as he took deliberate steps back up to the pulpit.

"You have a wonderful pastor here at Old Dominion. Do you know that?"

At those words, applause sprang quickly from the audience. Tom Osborn had only been at Old Dominion United Methodist for eight months, but the young, red-haired, athletic pastor had already won the hearts of his congregation. Reverend Osborn had made a concerted effort to visit each family in its home within the first six months of his pastorate. He even took notes as families talked about their own history at Old Dominion, past operations and misfortunes, and personal testimonies.

"But as wonderful as Tom is," the evangelist resumed, "your pastor can't have near the influence for Christ you can have with your friends and work associates. When Tom mentions Jesus or invites people to your church, they consider that he is just doing what he's paid for. Then they will do their best to tell him what he wants to hear and never follow through. You, on the other hand, are seen as going out of your way to share something important to you. Tom's biggest responsibility is to enable you to share your faith."

Reverend Springstead pulled back his suit jacket sleeve to reveal his watch and made an elaborate effort at discerning the time. "I know we're all good Methodists. So I'd better finish, so we can be done by eight o'clock." He smiled at the congregation. A few giggles slipped into the sanctuary air.

"During the next three nights of revival, I want to talk to you about turning your life inside out. We must train ourselves to not focus on us, but to concentrate on those that still need to hear Jesus's story.

"But that will be useless information to you if you've never become a Christian. If you've claimed Jesus's death on the cross as payment for your sins and turned to him as Lord, he lives in you. Without that power, you can't get your eyes off yourself for very long."

The evangelist walked to the altar rail. "As we sing our closing hymn, I invite you to come meet me here at the front if you want to receive Jesus tonight. And all of you, come back tomorrow night as we learn to turn ourselves inside out."

CHAPTER 2

Pastor Tom Osborn paused in his sermon preparation to reflect on the past few days. Revival always took something out of the host church. There were meals to prepare, special music to perform, and hospitality to be arranged for the visiting speaker. But in spite of the energy required, revival services were expected to change lives. How many people this week moved closer to God?

At the end of all four nights, Reverend Springstead had included an invitation to accept God's gift of salvation. A total of two souls were saved, which was a bit disappointing. Yet Tom had never seen a congregation so attentive to a speaker's presentation. Each night, people had been on the edge of their seats. Maybe change was on the way.

Tom Osborn knew that his own life would never be the same. William Springstead had challenged them to turn their lives inside out, to get their minds off themselves. Tom didn't consider himself self-centered, but he seldom completely forgot himself in service to others. What would it be like to really keep others first in his thinking?

Professor Clinton used to tell his seminary classes, "Leadership is about more than training people. You've got to cheer them on. Be an encourager."

❧

In another part of Belton, John and Betty Carter sat at breakfast. Now that both of their boys were grown and had families of their own, meals together were very much like dating again. Today they found their conversation pulled inexorably to the subject of living "inside out."

"I don't think a person can really think of others first," John said. "Humans are built with an urge to survive. Self-preservation is what we're wired for."

His petite wife pushed a brunette lock of hair out of her face and gazed through the window, not actually seeing the beautiful day outside. "I'm sure it's not easy, dear," she said. "But the preacher made a pretty convincing argument that God expects that of us. Think about Mr. Miller at the post office."

"Mr. Miller? What about Mr. Miller?"

Betty put down her glass of orange juice and looked her tall husband in the eye. "Our postmaster always asks us how we're doing, and it's not small talk. He really wants to know. He never talks about himself. He seems to have that inside-out way of thinking."

"Hmm. Mr. Miller does it so naturally," John replied. "Okay. I'm going to give it a shot today."

On his way to work, John Carter stopped at Bestmart. The giant discount store was bustling with activity, even at 8:15 a.m. John quickly found the razor blades and legal pads he needed and headed for the checkout lanes.

In spite of all the registers at the front of the store, only two lanes were open. "This is what Bestmart is famous for," he grumbled to himself.

John chose one of the lines. The shopper in front of him was just beginning to put his purchases on the counter. What a load! He had at least thirty cartons of soft drinks in the shopping cart.

Another shopper lined up behind John. The blue-jeaned young mother and her toddler daughter had a pretty big load too. *I'm sure glad I got in line before them*, he thought. *I'd surely be late for work.*

The little girl was whining a little now, begging to be allowed to open the box of fish-shaped crackers in her little hands.

"Wait until they're paid for, Betsy," her mother scolded.

John suddenly remembered the little phrase from revival. *Think inside out.*

A voice in his head spoke to John. *Let the mother and her daughter ahead of you in line.*

He glanced at the two items in his hands, then snuck a look at the full shopping cart behind him. This was hard.

Ahead of him, the adept cashier had breezed through the cart with the soft drinks by scanning one carton over and over, and it was almost his turn to be checked out.

"Ma'am," John said to the young mother, "why don't you go ahead of me? I've got plenty of time." He tried to smile big enough to make her believe it.

With a look of shock, the mother replied, "Are you sure?"

John nodded vigorously, smiled, and with a sweep of his arm indicated that they were welcome to move ahead. He quickly stepped behind them in line, and mother and daughter began unloading the full shopping cart.

John kept the smile pasted on his face. He glanced at his watch. The phrase *I am going to be late* ran through his mind, to the tune of "Twinkle, Twinkle, Little Star." *I am going to be late.*

"Sir, I'm opening up. I can take you over here," a voice called out from a nearby lane. John turned his head to see a smiling Bestmart cashier looking his way. He hurried to take her up on the offer.

He finished checking out before the young mother had her cart halfway emptied.

What just happened? John asked himself.

CHAPTER 3

Tom Osborn and John and Betty Carter were not the only persons thinking about "living inside out." Not nearly. Out of sixty regular attenders at Old Dominion, about a dozen were still grappling with the message from last week's revival.

Ricky Temple grappled with more than just revival. He struggled with a life in a mess.

Thirty-four years ago, Ricky had slept through his first worship service at Old Dominion United Methodist, carried there by loving parents on his tenth day of life. He had slept through many more church services in the intervening years, and those that he stayed awake for had left no impression.

Short, muscular, and handsome, Ricky loved to spend time with his friends, but he never missed church. It always kept him on the good side of his parents. Since revival though, church had taken on new meaning.

"Jesus can give you the power to turn your life inside out. But until you have Jesus as your Savior, you can't even turn your life right side up!" Reverend Springstead had said.

The preacher was right. Ricky needed to get his life straightened up. So he walked the aisle last Tuesday night and gave control of all he was to Jesus.

And now, the tangle that represented his life was slowly being unknotted.

The letter was addressed to "Pastor, Old Dominion UMC." The return address was 414 Beattie Road in Helmsville. Tom set it aside for a moment, while he sorted through catalogs and requests from independent ministries. It occurred to him that wastebaskets filled up quicker every year.

Tom slit open the letter from Helmsville. "Dear Tom," it started, "I just discovered that you serve a church only sixteen miles from where my parents and I live. I'll take a Sunday off from my children's ministry job at Calvary Baptist soon, and come hear you preach. It will be great to see you again. In His service, Sylvia Beattie."

He stared at the letter, frozen in his hand. He could feel his heart pounding.

Sylvia was the only other redhead in his seminary that first year, so naturally she caught his eye. She never seemed to be in any of his classes, but the few times he got to see her, he was impressed with her smile and easy laughter.

At one time he thought he had a crush on her, but decided he must not be studying enough. She graduated after he'd been in seminary one year.

She must still be single, since she lived with her parents.

"Coming back for the Hawks game tonight, Ricky?" Ben Williams called out from the other end of the bar.

Ben, Keith Slappey, and Ricky were regulars at Freddy's Sports Pub. The three close friends could be found every Monday through Friday, right after work, at the popular sports bar.

"I don't know, Ben. Maybe not. I promised myself I'd make some time for a little introspection. The Hawks are going to swallow the Cavaliers whole, whether I watch the game or not. I might as well do something constructive."

"Think your mirror can stand you staring at it for a couple hours?" Keith asked.

"Heck, we're not talking hours, we're talking minutes," Ben said, smoothing his straight-back blond hair. Chuckles erupted from several nearby booths. "Ricky, maybe you could just step out the back door during timeouts. By the time the game is over, you'll be all squared away."

Ricky grinned. That's what he liked about his friends here at the pub. They never let you take yourself too seriously.

"Hey, guys," Ricky said. "I've really got to get a hold on stuff. My life is a mess. I'm not getting anywhere. I can't see myself working in sporting goods at Bestmart the rest of my life. I live in a tiny apartment, I'm not married, I've got no savings, and I feel like God's got bigger plans for me. I need to get a life."

Silence reigned in Freddy's for the next half minute.

Keith was the next to speak. "Let me know what you hear from God, Ricky," he said as he headed for the door. "I could use some straightening out, myself. Maybe he can do 'two for the price of one.'"

Random drops of sweat fell from her forehead onto the gray basement floor. Something behind the television rattled with each movement, as Lydia strained to keep up with the lean exercise instructor on the DVD. Jump for jump, lunge for lunge, kick for kick—she stayed with the leader, all the way to the familiar "Good work, ladies! Now take a break and grab a bottle of water."

Lydia Michaelson turned off the TV and flopped down on the old wooden rocker, exhausted yet exhilarated. *That's enough for one day*, she said to herself. *That's about a half hour more exercise than any other 84-year-old in Belton got today.*

Her mind wandered to some of the other senior citizens in Old Dominion church. Most had several doctors that they visited regularly. She only had Dr. Fungo, whom she visited once a year for a checkup. Other older men and women took a dozen or more pills every day; she refused to take any.

Lydia worked hard to take care of herself. After all, wasn't her body the temple of the Holy Spirit? Their young pastor, Tom Osborn, would remind them of that verse fairly often.

Since the revival, Lydia had a certain unsettled feeling creeping in. She was faithful to attending church, she read her Bible daily, and she tithed. But was she thinking about others? In her determination to stay healthy, Lydia spent most of her time focused on herself.

CHAPTER 4

He didn't even notice the birds any more.
Parrots, toucans, and macaws roosted everywhere in Susan's Wild Bird Coffee Shop. Red, green, blue, and yellow splashed their most vibrant hues around the place. At least thirty of the brightly colored jungle birds lived in the establishment.

Lived? None of the birds was actually alive, but they were colorful reproductions of the real thing.

Reverend Tom Osborn sat down in his usual place, third table from the door. Immediately he flipped open his laptop computer and continued working on Sunday's sermon from the book of Jonah.

"Good morning, Preacher Tom, I'm glad you're here," said Helen Adams, the shop's petite blond waitress. "Regular coffee today, or would you care to try our special Jalapeno Dark? I think you told me once that hot peppers are your favorite vegetable."

"Wow," Tom replied, "that sounds great! Is it spicy?"

"Not really. Most of the jalapeno is in the aroma. But we don't sell the aroma separate."

"Bring me a sixteen-ounce cup, I guess."

"Bagel and cream cheese?"

"As usual. I've got to have my bagel every day."

Helen eased away to fill his breakfast order. Tom returned to his laptop and his next sermon on the reluctant prophet, Jonah.

In the book of Jonah, chapter one, Jonah asked the sailors to throw him into the sea, so the storm would abate. They did, reluctantly, and the sea grew calm. Then the sailors worshipped Jonah's God.

"Amazing," Tom accidentally said aloud, then to himself, *Jonah gave his life that others might live. That's really living "inside out." How much am I giving of myself that others might find a better life?*

Suddenly the smell of jalapeno invaded Tom's nostrils, grabbing his attention like an alarm.

"Here's your coffee, Tom. Kind of noticeable, isn't it?" Helen was there at his left elbow. "Your bagel is almost ready."

"Helen, while you're here, let me ask you something," he said. You know the story of Jonah and the whale, right?"

"Well, yeah. I haven't been to church much," she answered, "but everybody knows about Jonah."

"The reason he was in the sea for the fish to swallow him was because he told the sailors on the boat to throw him overboard and the storm would be calmed," Tom said. "It worked, and they worshipped God because it got their attention. What would it take today for church people to get the attention of the world around them?"

"You're asking me?" Helen replied. "Let me think a minute. Your bagel's up."

Tom Osborne turned back to his keyboard. *I can't ask my congregation to throw themselves off a boat*, he mused. *Still, we're not attracting notice by meeting behind closed doors a couple times a week. We've got to stick our necks out somehow and depend on God to do more than we could do ourselves.*

The coffee was really good. It had all the familiar flavor of hot jalapeno peppers without the fire and the crunch. He'd have to get a refill.

The waitress arrived with the pastor's morning bagel, accompanied by two packets of cream cheese. "To answer your question, I think people want, first of all, to see church people smiling, like going to church has made a difference in their lives. A lot of them look so stern and rigid. And then they've got to help people, not just live for themselves and walk right by people in need. If I'm going to go to the trouble of asking for a Sunday off to go to some church, I want to know it's going to be worth it."

Another customer came through the door. Helen greeted her with a big smile and said, "Good morning. I'm glad you're here." Turning back to Reverend Osborn, she said, "Thanks for asking."

On Sunday morning, just before the benediction, Tom Osborn paused and looked down. He had everybody's attention. Several seconds passed as they waited for their pastor to reveal whatever it was he was pondering.

"Friends," he finally said, "I still can't get off my mind what our guest revival speaker left us with more than a week ago. We've got to think inside out. I'm convinced it's the difference between our church growing and just staying the same. If you're in the same boat as I am, and you're trying to begin living inside out, let's meet at the Pancake House tonight after church and talk about it. Maybe we can share our experiences and encourage each other.

"All right. Please bow for the benediction."

After most of the congregation had filed past the pastor, exchanging pleasantries and praising him for a good sermon, Lydia Michaelson took Tom's hand and pulled him down to whisper in his ear.

"I'll be at the Pancake House tonight, and it's on me. I'm paying for everybody's meal."

As Lydia stepped away, he felt an arm slip inside his. He turned to see a smiling young lady with flaming red hair. "Can I take you to lunch?"

Her laughter rang through the lobby, and Tom Osborn gave Sylvia his biggest hug of the day.

CHAPTER 5

In spite of the Sunday lunch crowd, the hostess at Santini's instinctively knew to look for a table in a quiet corner for the young couple.

"Sylvia, how did I manage to miss seeing you in the congregation this morning? I'm always looking out for visitors."

Sylvia winked. "I've been in church all my life, and I know the tricks. I slipped in during a prayer, and sat behind some large people. I was worried you'd see my hair, and I wouldn't be able to surprise you."

"No, you totally surprised me. But in a happy way. So you work in a church?"

"Yes. When I graduated from seminary, a friend in Helmsville told me Calvary Baptist was thinking of hiring someone to work with the children. I talked the Board of Deacons into giving me a part-time position as their first Children's Minister, on trial. They only had fifteen kids at the time, but I built the program up, and now it's a full-time position. We have over seventy children under sixth grade."

"Wow. Sounds like you brought in a lot of young families. I'll bet you could name your salary."

The waiter came for their order. Sylvia and Tom both ordered lasagna, along with coffee and a salad.

"I wish the salary was a little higher, but, hey, my expenses are low. Mom and Dad charge me room and board, but they won't let me give them more than a hundred dollars a month."

The waiter slipped their coffee mugs onto the table. "I'll be right back with your salads."

Sylvia said, "So tell me about Old Dominion. It seems like a nice little church, but I got the impression they aren't used to welcoming many visitors."

"Uh oh. Did somebody say something?"

"Oh, no, it just seemed people were overly happy to see me."

Tom proceeded to tell her about his months at Old Dominion, the stagnation lately, and the beginning signs of progress since the revival services.

"I've been trying to change the way I do ministry," Tom said. "At Red Oaks, my first church, I did a lot of the work myself. They encouraged that, so I could learn how to do ministry. But now, I've got to be more of an encourager, a cheerleader."

"It worked for me," said Sylvia.

"By the way, whatever happened to Rob Smith, the guy I used to see you with at seminary?"

"He's a pastor in Texas now. You did know that he's my cousin, right?"

"No, I don't think I ever knew that."

"Well," said Sylvia, "that explains a few things!" She laughed as if it were the funniest thing she'd heard in days.

Hank Walton stretched his long legs and let his mind wander through recent events while he waited for his Sunday lunch at Susan's Wild Bird Coffee Shop. Five years ago, he could never have imagined he'd be a 66-year-old widowed retiree raising a pretty, 12-year-old granddaughter.

Life had changed so fast. Three years ago, their divorced daughter had died in a car accident on the way to work. Hank and Jeanette took custody of Mandy when her father, recently remarried, refused to take the child into his home, and they immediately took steps to legally adopt their granddaughter.

A year and a half ago, tragedy struck again. His beloved Jeanette died of pneumonia, and Hank and Mandy were left alone. They clung to each other, as if they were the last two people on earth.

How in the world would he be able to raise a near-teenage girl on his own? Hank knew little about the styles of clothing young girls wore, or how to talk to Mandy about dating, or what kind of cell phone she really needed, or how she should fix her hair.

He missed his wife terribly. Jeanette would be able to handle all these female things.

The church had been extremely helpful. Old Dominion had a good youth group, about a dozen strong, and parents of Mandy's friends in the group would invite her to spend the weekend with them a couple times a month.

And then there was Rita Johnson. Rita was a forty-year-old, pony-tailed accountant, never married, who somehow had struck up a friendship with Mandy. They really hit it off. Rita and Mandy acted like two college roommates when they were together. It was just uncanny.

"Here's your ham and cheese on rye, Hank," Helen, the waitress, said. "Need more coffee?"

"Yes, please," Hank replied. "Thank you, Helen."

God had planted an idea in Hank's head three months ago, one of those thoughts so wild and wondrous that it was absolutely stunning. Why not invite Rita to come live with them?

The idea seemed foolish at first, but it would not go away. The five-bedroom house was certainly big enough for another person. Rita was a sincere Christian. Most of all, Mandy needed a woman in the house.

Lord, are you sure?

Tom Osborn requested the small room in the back at the Pancake House, not really knowing how many of his parishioners would show up. Were there three or four of them trying to live "inside out," or a lot more?

John and Betty Carter were there already. Lydia Michaelson had promised to pay for the meal, so certainly she'd walk through the door any minute.

Ricky Temple came in, but he had a slim, blond friend with him that the pastor didn't recognize. They just happened to be at the same restaurant, he guessed. No, he heard Ricky ask where the group from Old

Dominion Church was meeting. *Nothing wrong with bringing a guest*, he thought.

Hank Walton entered the room just after Lydia.

"Hank, good to see you," John Carter called out. "Where is your lovely granddaughter tonight?"

"She and Rita went to play miniature golf right after Mandy got out of youth group. Have you ever seen two friends as close?" John smiled and shook his head.

The waiter slipped in and asked, "Are you all ready to order?"

Tom glanced toward the door and said, "I think we're all here. Eddie, I'll just have coffee and two of your tremendous strawberry pancakes."

The waiter proceeded around the table, gathering orders, and then left for the kitchen.

"Ricky," Tom said, "how about introducing your guest? Then we'll each say our name, and tell something about how we're doing with 'inside-out' living."

"Sure." Ricky agreed. "This is Keith Slappey, and we've been friends a long time."

After everyone greeted Keith, Ricky continued. "I'm Ricky Temple. On the Tuesday night of revival, I asked God to take control of my life, and I feel like he's really taking hold of me. I'm starting to see how self-centered I've been."

Betty spoke next. "My name is Betty Carter. We pray for a long list of people in our Sunday school class each week. To live 'inside out,' I've started writing a short note to each one, just to encourage them and say we're praying for them."

"That's a great idea," Lydia said. "I always think I'm going to do that, but I never get around to it."

After John Carter followed with his story about standing in line at Bestmart, the waiter arrived with their food. For the next several minutes, much of the conversation was replaced by the click and clack of forks on plates.

During a quiet moment, Keith spoke up. "I don't know a lot about this 'inside-out' stuff yet, but Ricky seems to be straightening out his life. I want what he's got. Help me find it."

CHAPTER 6

It was a great first meeting for those interested in living inside out. They decided to call themselves the Inside-Out Project. It was agreed they would meet every other Sunday night after church.

Keith Slappey made the biggest impression, by asking how to get whatever it was that had turned his friend Ricky Temple's life around.

"Keith," Betty Carter said, "I've known Ricky all his life. Just going to church didn't give him the power to live right, any more than getting into your car gets you to work. You've got to find the key and start your engine."

Her husband, John, added, "Everybody has heard that Jesus died on the cross a couple thousand years ago, but until you understand and believe that he died to pay the penalty for your own disobedience to God, your sin, you won't have God's Spirit living in you to give you power for your everyday life."

"All right, let me see if I understand," Keith said. "My friend, Ricky, believed that the death of Jesus paid for his past wrongdoing. That's all that God required, for Ricky to be in right standing with him, and now God works with him every day to fly right. What am I missing here? It can't be that easy."

Hank spoke up. "People have tried since the beginning of time to be good on their own willpower, but it just can't be done. We need someone to save us, to pay a price we can't pay, and Jesus is it."

Keith was silent for a bit, obviously chewing on what had been said.

"Keith," Ricky said, "remember those signs people used to bring to football games? 'John 3:16' would show up at every game. That's a verse out of the Bible that says it all for me: 'For God so loved the world that he gave his only Son, that whosoever believes in him should not perish, but have everlasting life.'"

"So it really is that easy?" Keith asked. "I just tell God, from my heart, that I believe Jesus died to pay for my sins, and God will live with me every day to make my life better? Man, what a deal! I'm ready! Tell me what to say."

"Let's all do this together," Pastor Osborn said. "We'll all close our eyes and pray. Keith, you just repeat after me what I say to God."

Tom prayed a prayer of repentance with Keith, and the whole group applauded after the "amen."

"I feel a little different," Keith said, "like I'm starting on a major adventure. You all help me along, okay?"

Everyone present pledged to do just that.

Hank Walton did not share with the group what God was telling him about Rita. If he asked Rita to move in with them and she refused, he'd rather nobody else ever knew about it. But he decided he would ask her soon.

Lydia Michaelson left the meeting feeling energized. The best way to learn to live inside out was to just do it! Monday morning, Lydia would do something for somebody else. Her focus was coming off Lydia.

At nine o'clock the next morning, Tom Osborn heard a rap on his office door.

"Good morning!" he called out. "Please come in."

"Good morning, Tom," Lydia said as she entered. She was carrying an overloaded small cardboard box. "I need your help," she added.

"Well, Lydia, the church rummage sale is still a couple months away," he said. "Let's put that box in the storage room in the fellowship hall."

Lydia drilled Tom with her hazel eyes. "Pastor, this is for that young man that got saved last night. I can't recall Keith's last name. It sounded like he might need some guidance in what he's supposed to do next, so I gathered up a few things."

Lydia put her box down on the edge of Tom's desk and proceeded to empty the contents, one item at a time.

"Sounds like he may not own a Bible. I brought a New King James and a Contemporary English Version. I also put in *My Utmost for His Highest*, by Oswald

Chambers. Here's a couple CDs, one by Sandi Patty and a Chris Tomlin one.

"He probably needs some kind of commentary to explain the Bible, so I'm giving him my *Halley's Bible Handbook*. I'll get a new one, next time I order from Amazon. And I wanted him to have this little foot-tall desk cross, as a reminder of what Jesus did for him."

"Wow, that's all great, Lydia," Tom said. "How are you going to get it all to Keith?"

"Why, pastor," she replied. "That's your job."

The pastor gave Lydia his biggest smile. "Maybe it will mean more to Keith if you deliver this package, just because it's not your job. And make sure he knows we want him to come to Old Dominion this Sunday."

CHAPTER 7

H ank Walton wound down to the end of his prayer time.

"And Lord, help me to do your will. You've made it clear to me that you want me to invite Rita to come live with Mandy and me. But it seems selfish to me, and I'm trying to live for others, to live inside out. Rita living here would help me in raising Mandy, and that just seems selfish, like I'm solving my own problems. Settle my mind, dear Father. Help me see Rita's side. Is there any benefit for her?"

Betty Carter finally got her husband off to work. Now she could get started on the shrubbery.

At times she missed teaching fifth grade at C.G. Smith Elementary, but, really, those times were rare. Every year, the students were taller, a little less polite, less disciplined, and less likely to keep up with her pace. It all combined to make her feel less and less in control.

Here in her yard, she could be in charge. Today, she would cut back those gangly crepe myrtles, then cut up and plant a row of red seed potatoes in her thirty-by-twenty-foot garden patch.

One of the things Betty liked best about gardening was giving fresh vegetables away to her neighbors. That really fit in with the little movement she was part of at the church, "living inside out." She and John probably gave away a tenth of what their garden produced.

She wondered how John would feel about increasing their generosity to half of their vegetables.

❧

Hank didn't recognize the number on the caller ID screen on his phone, but he decided to answer anyway. He'd never known telemarketers to call in the morning.

"Hello?" he spoke into the telephone.

"Hello, Hank? This is Rita Johnson," the voice responded.

Hank could feel himself getting slightly nervous. What was it he had asked of God this morning concerning Rita?

"Good morning, Rita," he said. "Are you calling from work, or is this a day off?"

"Oh, don't I wish," she replied. "Any days off will have to wait until after tax season. I'd just be glad to get back to a forty-hour week."

"Did I forget to send you something you needed for preparing my tax return?"

"Actually, Hank, I'm not calling about anything to do with work," Rita said. "Could you meet me for lunch? I think it's time we chatted together about Mandy."

Hank thought, *Lord, are you up to something?*

"Rita, I think I can work you into my schedule," he said into the phone. "I'm in the middle of…nothing. It's nice being retired."

She laughed. He could hear a thimble-full of stress being released. People should laugh more.

"Do you know where Freddy's Sports Pub is?" Rita replied. "I'm not a drinker, but they've got great sandwiches, and it's not too crowded. Let's meet at noon."

Hank entered the dimly-lit neighborhood bar and grill and immediately saw Rita Johnson's hand wave to him from a corner booth. A waiter followed him to the table, requesting his drink order.

"Iced tea, please," Hank told the waiter. "Rita?" She raised her glass, indicating she'd already been served.

"I'm glad you could meet me on such short notice, Hank," she said. "The burgers are good, but I always get the turkey sub. If I don't take care of myself, nobody else will," she added, with a smile.

When the waiter returned with Hank's tea, he told the young man, "I'll have what Rita's having, please."

"That would be two turkey subs with salad then, with avocado and sunflower kernels and our raspberry vinaigrette," the waiter replied. "Won't take but a minute."

After the waiter left, Rita said, "I thought you'd be the burger type."

"I can eat most anything," Hank said. "My cholesterol and blood pressure have never given me any problems. I just don't eat much dessert any more."

Rita seemed to be searching for a starting point.

"Rita," Hank proceeded, "you said you wanted to chat about Mandy. Thank you for spending time with her. You know there's no female influence at my house, so I'm glad for every lady that steps in to help. There's going to be a lot I don't know about raising a girl in our present day. My own daughter, Mandy's mother, left our house nearly twenty years ago."

"Mandy is a wonderful young lady," Rita said. "She's so grown up. She seems to think of me more as a girlfriend than a forty-year-old adult. It's refreshing for me. We have a lot of fun together."

Out of the corner of his eye, Hank saw somebody heading their way. Their lunch arrived.

Talk suspended for a few minutes, as Hank and Rita worked on their salads and subs.

"Hank," Rita resumed. "Mandy has been asking me to come spend the night with her sometime. I didn't know if I should. Would you be embarrassed to have a woman sleeping in your house? I mean, you're old enough to be my...Well, I wouldn't want people to think, you know, you and me..."

Rita's face had turned a brilliant shade of red.

CHAPTER 8

Hank's hearty laughter rescued Rita from her embarrassment.

"I guess it would look a little funny," he said. "I'm so naive, I just thought of your visit as my daughter having a friend over. Technically, my granddaughter is also my legally adopted daughter."

Rita ventured, "Then you think it would be okay for me to accept your daughter's invitation?"

Hank smiled. "Rita, I want Mandy to have friends over to her house, just like any other girl her age would do. You are welcome any time."

For a few moments, Hank and Rita let conversation lag, as they gave their food renewed attention. He carefully nibbled at the avocado; it looked a little strange, but he considered himself not too old to try something new.

Rita picked up the conversation again. "I would invite Mandy to my condo, but I'm not really happy with the environment there anymore. It seems I've acquired neighbors who have a loud party two or three nights a week. I'm seriously thinking of moving."

Hank replied, "You'd like our neighborhood. It's a quiet, family-friendly area. The wildest party lately was a five-year-old's birthday party down the street."

Rita laughed. "That's more my speed. If I could find a little place in your neighborhood, I'd be a lot closer to my job too. If you hear of anything, please keep me in mind."

Hank was just about to speak, when Rita looked at her watch. "Oh! I forgot. I've got to stop at the cleaners on my way back to work. You'll have to excuse me, Hank."

She quickly rose from the table. As she turned to leave, he called out her name.

"Rita," he said. "I enjoyed it. Have a nice afternoon. Lunch is on me."

❧

A few hours later, also at Freddy's Sports Pub, Ricky Temple and Keith Slappey sat sipping their after-work beers.

"Ricky," Keith said, "you read the Bible much?"

"Not 'til lately," he answered. "Since I put God in charge of my life, I've been reading some to remind myself how I'm supposed to live. After being in church all these years, I ought to know what to do, but I guess I wasn't paying attention."

Keith offered, "Somebody told me at work that I'd have to quit drinking. I tried to look it up, but I just found the part about Jesus drinking wine with the guys at that supper the night before he was killed."

"I wonder if he would have drunk light beer if they had it back then," Ricky said. "Anyway, we're supposed to go to the entire world to share what God has done for us. This place needs us. Ever see the preacher in here?"

Hank finished washing dishes Friday night just as his granddaughter, Mandy, came into the kitchen. She threw her arms around him and gave him a big hug.

"I love you, Granddaddy," Mandy said, beaming up at him.

"I love you, too, angel," he replied. She was certainly growing! Even at six foot four, he was less than a foot taller than Mandy.

As she released him, she asked, "Is it okay if I have a friend over tomorrow night?"

Hank smiled. "Any time you want to invite somebody over, it's all right with me. Just remember to tell them to bring church clothes for Sunday. Is it anybody I know?"

"Just Rita, Granddaddy," she answered. "She wants to show me some ways to fix my hair. Then we're gonna play games and watch a movie. Granddaddy, I want to be a blond. What do you think?"

That caught him by surprise. Mandy's hair was the same light brunette color that her mother's had been.

"Hmm. I never thought of you as Mandy, the blond," Hank said. "Have you considered blue, or a fiery red?"

His granddaughter laughed. "Ooh, yuck. I don't think I'd like either one of those," she said.

"Well, I'll tell you what," Hank said. "Let's ask Rita when she gets here tomorrow. I've never been a blond. All I've ever been is black or gray."

❧

Ricky Temple pulled his Ford Focus out of the parking lot at Freddy's and headed home.

"Weekend! I thought it would never get here," he said to himself. He had an extra beer at Freddy's to celebrate.

Ricky headed out Fairfax Drive, Belton's main highway leaving downtown. A block ahead, he could see a pedestrian start to cross the four-lane.

By the time his Focus got to the corner, the man had barely made it to the center of the street. As Ricky passed, the pedestrian whipped his head around, surprised at how close the car had come to him.

Why didn't I slow down? Ricky chided himself. *Was it that extra beer? If it had been me, I'd have been scared. But I was only thinking of myself.*

CHAPTER 9

Universally, pastors take stock on Monday mornings. Tom had learned in seminary that most resignations by pastors happen on Mondays, usually because pastors misread the mood of the congregation on Sunday.

He had never had a "down" Monday at Old Dominion United Methodist Church. His congregation was always affirming and eager to grow closer to God.

Tom could see changes in his flock since revival. Giving was up, both to the general budget and to missions. Members visibly cared more about one another. Sunday school attendance was up. Reverend Springstead's revival theme, "living inside out," had become a catchphrase.

The aspect of evangelism was missing though. Shouldn't a person living for others be sharing the good news? Telling people how God has changed your life is not bragging, or at least it shouldn't be. It should be more like one needy person telling another where to find help.

John Carter arrived at his desk in the Loss Control Department of Edison Fund Insurance a good bit before the 8:45 starting time. He hoped to have time to chat with his coworkers.

John was known as a hard worker who kept to himself. That had to change. God was calling him to live for others, inside out.

"Morning, John," a stout brunette said as she passed his desk.

"Good morning, Becky," he replied. "Did you have a good weekend?"

"Most of it, I guess," she said. "My son Jason fell out of a tree yesterday afternoon and broke his leg. We spent about four hours in the emergency room. Up until then, it was a great weekend."

John could tell that Becky really needed to tell someone the whole ordeal, and with very little coaxing, she did.

A few minutes later, as Becky was leaving for her own desk, John said, "I'll be sure to pray for Jason, Becky. Every day."

She smiled and said, "I appreciate it."

John grabbed his purple coffee cup from the right rear corner of his desk and headed for the break room. On the way back, he passed Fred Smith's desk. The young manager trainee was scrawling a list of words in very large print on a yellow pad.

"Good morning, Fred," John said. "You seem mighty busy for eight forty in the morning."

When Fred glanced up, beads of perspiration dotted his forehead.

"Good morning, Mr. Carter," the slim young man replied.

"Call me John," John Carter said.

"Good morning, John. Yeah, I've got a presentation for my department at nine," Fred said. "First time. I'm kind of nervous."

"Tell you what, Fred," John said. "I'll say a prayer for you. Always works."

John Carter headed back to his desk. It was nearly 8:45 a.m. and the beginning of the work day.

From twenty feet away, Fred Smith called out, "Always?"

John smiled and nodded.

Sylvia was relieved to know why Tom had kept her at arms' length at seminary. He assumed her cousin was her boyfriend. Now that the matter was cleared up, she hoped they might get to know each other better.

Tonight he was taking her to dinner and then a movie in Helmsville. She tried to keep in mind that a pastor was always on call. She prayed that everyone at Old Dominion United Methodist Church would be happy and well tonight.

"Surely I'm not running out of money," Lydia Michaelson said to herself. She rarely heard from her lawyer and financial advisor, Franklin Morris. He made it clear he wanted to see her soon.

"Good morning, Ms. Michaelson," the receptionist said as Lydia entered.

"Good morning, Sarah," Lydia replied. "It's good to see a familiar face. I believe you're the only person who was here the day I became Franklin's client."

"Oh dear, has it been that long since your father died?" she said. "Graham Michaelson was such a fine man. Let me tell Franklin you're here."

Sarah slipped to the back and returned immediately to summon Lydia to her employer's office.

After Lydia was seated and they had exchanged greetings, Franklin closed his office door.

"Lydia," Franklin began, "I've been crunching some numbers. At the present rate you're spending, do you have any idea when you will run out of spending money?"

Though the attorney sounded serious, he had sprouted a wide grin.

"Well," Lydia answered, "I was hoping to have enough to support me until I'm one hundred."

"Not even close," he answered. His grin widened.

"Try two hundred. Or three hundred. Lydia, I really don't think you will ever run out." Franklin Morris took a seat behind his desk.

She didn't quite know what to say next. She was careful to never spend more than her Social Security check each month, and she just had her pension from the power company deposited in a savings account each month. The pension would only be used for major purchases, like a car or a new roof.

"You have not read the semiannual statements from your daddy's stock portfolio that I've been sending you, have you?" he said. "That little bit of stock he had in the soft drink giant and the supplemental insurance company is now worth over five million dollars."

A shriek escaped from her lips. No other words would come.

"And," he went on, "your closest heir is so distant that she has probably never heard of you. We need to talk about philanthropy."

CHAPTER 10

"Hello, Hank?" Rita Johnson said. "I was going to take Mandy over to Belton College this afternoon to see a little Picasso exhibit they've got this month. Did she ask you about it?"

"Good morning, Rita," Hank said. "Yes, she mentioned it at breakfast this morning. That's fine with me. Mandy said the exhibit was just Wednesday and today."

"I don't suppose you've heard of any houses or apartments opening up in the neighborhood, have you? My partying neighbors are getting louder every week. I've got to get out of here."

Hank Walton took a deep breath.

"Actually, something may be developing along those lines," he said. "How about stopping by for lunch and we can talk about it? I made some chicken salad last night, and I've got some blueberries and cantaloupe."

"Is it a house or an apartment?" Rita sounded excited.

Hank just said, "See you at noon?"

"That's all you're going to tell me, isn't it?" Rita sighed. "I'll be there at noon."

❧

Betty walked in the door and then stopped, still as a mannequin. What had she walked into?

There were birds everywhere! Three parrots perched in a tree just five feet to her right. Two macaws and a toucan sat on a pipe over the cash register. Another jungle bird perched atop a lamp in the corner to her left. Had she gotten the wrong door, or was this really a coffee shop?

Someone called out, "Good morning, I'm glad you're here!" About twenty feet away, a young, blond waitress smiled warmly.

The smell of coffee was definitely in the air. Small tables, with two or four chairs, were randomly spaced about the room.

At a nearby table, a short, white-haired lady began to laugh at her. Betty's first reaction was to get angry, but she told herself, *Think inside out*, and realized she probably did look comical.

The waitress, whose name tag said Helen, touched her arm and said, "Ma'am, the birds aren't real. You look so puzzled!"

Betty laughed heartily, and everyone else joined in.

"I thought I'd walked into a pet store," Betty said to the white-haired lady.

The woman stood up and extended her hand. "I'm Susan, the owner of the birds and this little cafe. Yes, you certainly looked confused for a moment. I couldn't help but laugh. Now, how about some coffee? Welcome to Susan's Wild Bird Coffee Shop."

Rita Johnson's black BMW pulled into Hank's driveway just a couple minutes past noon. He took the chicken salad and fruit from the kitchen counter and placed them next to the pita bread on the kitchen table.

"Do I need to come in, or do we need to go look at the house first?" Rita said.

"Oh, please come in," Hank said. "Lunch is on the table. Water or decaf iced tea?"

"Just water, please, Hank," she said, as she seated herself in her familiar chair. "I really enjoyed being here with Mandy last weekend. You know, you're quite the cook."

After Hank gave thanks to God for the food, he said, "We really enjoyed having the company. It's a big house for just two people."

"How big is it?" she asked. "I think we spent the whole weekend in Mandy's room and the den."

"And the bathroom, making my granddaughter a blond," he added. "Rita, we've got ten rooms plus four and a half baths. Jeanette and I got a bargain at the time we bought the house, but it's always been more than we needed. We could take in a boarder and still have plenty of room."

"You certainly could have three people in this big house. A third of it is as large as my condo."

Hank paused and abruptly turned all his attention to his lunch.

Rita said, "So where in this neighborhood is the apartment you were telling me about earlier? I'd love to see it."

Hank took another big bite of lunch. Rita waited patiently while he chewed.

Hank picked up his pita and took another big bite. Rita was surprised at his rude behavior.

Then it hit her.

When her ability to form words returned a half minute later, Rita said, "Hank, I don't know. Let me pray about this, okay? I've never had a man ask me to move in with him before."

Hank couldn't help but laugh. "Think of it as moving in with good friends, Mandy and her grandfather."

❧

Before the benediction, Pastor Tom Osborn reminded the congregation of the biweekly meeting that night of the Inside-Out Project.

Then he said, "Now Lydia has asked for a moment to speak. Lydia?"

Lydia Michaelson strode purposefully to the pulpit. "Thank you, Pastor. I've got a surprise gift for you all today. Our ushers are now passing out a ten-dollar bill to each and every one of you. It's yours, I don't want it back."

Lydia paused a few seconds for effect.

"But," she went on, "there is a string attached. This money is not for you. I expect you to do something with it to help somebody else. And let's all bring back stories of how God used you to bless somebody else."

CHAPTER 11

"John, let's get lunch at someplace different today," Betty Carter said to her husband after church. "I found an incredible little coffee shop that serves a light lunch and great coffee. I know you'll like it."

"Okay," he said. "You know I hate to wash dishes on Sunday. Any place but home!"

Betty directed her husband to Simpson Street and Susan's Wild Bird Coffee Shop. As Betty expected, John was distracted by the colorful birds as they entered, but she deftly guided him to a table for two about fifteen feet into the building.

"Welcome!" Helen, the young waitress, called out. "Betty, I'm glad you're back. I guess you got over your shock from the other day."

Betty chuckled. "Did you see my husband's face when he entered? Same effect. John, this is Helen Adams. She's a recent grad with a business degree from Belton College."

"Nice to meet you, Helen," John said. "Are you looking to eventually get an MBA?"

"I'd really rather start a small business," Helen replied, "but I've got to save up some money first. Look, I know you guys are hungry. Let me get you a menu."

It only took a few minutes for their salads to arrive. As they ate, the Carters discussed the ten dollars they received in church.

"Betty," John said, "I'm going to buy a wooden box, or maybe a piggy bank. I'll put stick-on letters on it that say 'Prayer' and put it on my desk at work. More and more people are asking me to pray for them. It's a growing ministry."

"Lydia didn't give us a lot of direction, did she?" Betty said. "I like your idea. It will certainly bless other people, and any stories you hear of how those prayers are answered will encourage us all. Me, I'm thinking tomatoes."

John looked at his wife and waited. If he gave her half a chance, he knew she'd explain. He took another bite of lunch.

"The tomatoes in our salads are kind of...ordinary, aren't they?" Betty asked. "I enjoy giving away fresh-grown tomatoes in the summer. But I think I'd like to give somebody some tomato plants, to bless them even more."

Betty raised her hand to get the waitress's attention. Helen quickly made her way to their table.

"Helen, do you grow tomatoes?"

"I never really tried," she answered. "My daddy does, over in Montgomery, Alabama. There's nothing like a fresh tomato."

"I'm going to bring you a couple tomato plants tomorrow," Betty said. "Each one is in a five-gallon bucket. I'll tell you all you need to know to grow some big, juicy, tasty tomatoes."

Sunday night's meeting of the Inside-Out Project drew all seven charter members. After blessing their pancakes and other food, Tom began by saying, "Tell me how you've lived for others since our last meeting."

After several others related short incidents in which they had done a good turn for others, Hank spoke up.

"I took a big gamble on God this week," he began. "The Lord has been telling me for more than a month that I should invite a certain friend of my granddaughter's to come live with us. God was persistent with me. Finally, this week, I gave in."

It was not easy for Hank to trust these new friends with his story, but he sensed it was the right thing to do. He needed their prayers.

When he finished telling them about Rita's upcoming move, Hank said, "Please be careful who you tell about this. Some tongues may wag about an unmarried woman moving into my house. But I know this is God's way of taking care of Mandy."

Tom paused the meeting long enough for them to say a prayer for Hank.

After the "amen," Tom continued, "I hope you understand how important you are to me, and to God. This group is changing Old Dominion into a church that can grow. And it will. As you think of others first, you'll find that it's contagious. The best thing I can do, as your pastor, is to encourage you. I want to be your biggest fan. I want to have some kind of communication with each of you every week.

"Please be sure I've got your correct phone numbers and addresses on the clipboard before you leave. All right, is there anything else?"

Keith said, "Is there any place I shouldn't go with my story about the change Jesus made in my life?"

The group turned uncomfortably silent, though the wheels in each mind obviously turned at full speed.

Lydia spoke first. "Keith, there are some places I avoid as a Christian. But I think it's because I'm chicken."

Ricky said, "The Bible says to go to the entire world. Should we start with the places we really want to avoid? That might be where people need Jesus the most."

After several minutes of discussion, the pastor said, "I guess what we're saying is, go anywhere, but never go without preparing with prayer."

"And," John added, "the more Christian friends we make, the more we'll have to consciously seek places where non-Christians can be found."

"Make a list," Lydia asserted. "Plan new places to bring the good news. Where can I start going and get to know people that need Jesus in their lives?"

CHAPTER 12

How many of these books had he read? Hundreds. Maybe a thousand.

In his three years as the only full-time employee at The Book House, Keith Slappey had read an average of four or five books a week. Madge and Leo Randall, the owners, encouraged Keith to borrow any book he wanted to read, as long as he returned it promptly. He read like a starving man at a buffet.

The Book House carried current fiction best sellers, plus used books from fantasy to classics. On a good day, four hundred books sold.

"Excuse me, sir," called out a tall, blond man at the back of the store. "Have you got anything that reads like Clive Cussler? I've read everything he's written, and I've run out of anything to read."

Keith quickly headed in the man's direction.

"Yes sir, I can give you two or three good ideas," Keith replied. "There is one right by your right elbow."

After giving the man a few good leads on authors he might enjoy, Keith headed back to the front of the store.

"Keith," a lady in her forties said, "my daughter has read all the Hobbit books. What should I encourage her to read next that's in a similar vein?"

"Mrs. Castle," he said, "how about the Narnia books by C.S. Lewis?"

Keith paused for a second, unsure whether to venture into new territory. He never mentioned his faith at work.

"I've just reread the Narnia books," he continued. "I made some changes in my life recently, and I saw amazing Christian imagery in the Narnia books that I'd never seen before. It was like reading them for the first time. You might want to read them along with Christina, to make sure she doesn't miss anything."

Pastor Tom Osborn looked at his appointments for the day. It was four o'clock, and he had penciled in, "List outreach places."

As Lydia said last Sunday night, Christians need to go places where people need to hear about Jesus. Tom needed to adjust his lifestyle to add more of those places.

"All right," he said to himself, "I'm a young bachelor, working fairly regular hours. What kind of places do I need to go to?"

On a yellow legal pad, he wrote down a few places very quickly. Restaurants topped the list, since he didn't really like to cook. He needed gas for his car, a daily paper, a dry cleaner, auto repair, a grocery store, a bank. For most of these kinds of places, he already had a favorite one that he frequented, but he was not taking the time to get to know the workers.

For instance, he always used his debit card at the gas station and bought the daily paper outside, so he didn't yet know a single employee. Maybe he needed to buy his newspaper inside instead, and maybe even buy a soft drink or some chips, just to get to know the people that worked there.

He was feeling the need to get regular exercise, so he needed a gym to go to, or something like that. He also would eventually need a doctor and a dentist, but he didn't think he'd need an eye doctor any time soon.

Tom decided to make more of an effort to chat with people wherever he went. It was so easy to go through weeks without saying much at all to people that worked at businesses he used. The usual "How are you?" and "I'm fine," and "Have a nice day" did very little to develop relationships. He needed to notice name tags and remember what cashiers or waiters said about their families, even if he had to discreetly write it down.

Hadn't he promised himself he'd know everybody that lived on his street by now? What had happened to that idea? He had lived in Belton more than nine months, and he had only met the families that lived next door on both sides. *Come on, Tom*—he admonished himself—*live inside out!*

Rita closed all the windows, though the temperature outside was refreshing. The neighbors in the next condo were starting the party a little early tonight.

"I am so tired of this," she said out loud. "Lord, you know I need my sleep, and Hank and Mandy's neighborhood is so peaceful. If it's okay for me to move in with them, you're going to have to give me some kind of sign. I just don't know."

Even with the windows closed, Rita could still hear the music from next door. Was it her imagination, or were the walls vibrating?

After supper, Rita was washing dishes when the doorbell rang. She quickly dried her hands. Peeking through the peephole, she recognized the lady from the next condo and opened the door.

"Please come in," Rita said. "It's nice to see you again."

"I really can't stay, thank you," the tall lady in jeans replied. "We're entertaining my brother and his family tonight. By the way, you're always welcome to come join the party. My brother was just saying what a great condo we had, and he wondered if there might be another one of these he could buy. So I told him I'd go ask my neighbor, she's been here a while. Have you heard of anyone who might be looking to sell?"

CHAPTER 13

"So that's your prayer box, John?" Betty asked her husband.

John Carter held a large red pig in the crook of his arm. There was a large slot in the top; obviously, this ceramic animal had been originally manufactured as a coin bank. The stick-on letters on both sides proclaimed that it was now for "Prayers, Intercessions, Gratitude."

John smiled broadly. "I was looking for a simple box with a slot in the top. I couldn't find one anywhere. Then I suddenly saw this, and I decided that if I labeled it, it would serve quite well."

"So," Betty said, "you were in a store and this pig just jumped out at you."

"Yes, that's right," he replied. "Ambushed by a pig. Sounds like a crime, doesn't it?"

This section, she decided, could be called the parrot section. And she liked it here. The fake trees and flowers were just a little closer, making these two tables in the coffee shop almost like a nest.

As Betty waited for her coffee, she went through a mental list of what she wanted to get done this morning. She'd better make mulching the cucumbers a priority, or she'd be fighting weeds all summer. The red potatoes and buckets of tomatoes were coming along fine. Five hills of yellow squash and three of cucumbers would be plenty, but there was still a thirty-foot row that needed something. Flowers? Okra? Or maybe something she hadn't tried before.

"Need anything else?" Helen said as she slipped Betty's coffee onto the table. "We've got some fresh strawberry tarts you'd like."

"No, thanks, dear," Betty said. "How are your tomato plants coming along?"

"So far, so good," Helen answered. "You'll have to tell me when I need to do fertilizer and anything else. I really don't know about growing things."

Betty said, "I've got six other tomato plants in buckets, so whenever I do anything to them, I'll tell you, so you can do the same thing to yours. Right now, I just give them a good soaking of water every other day."

"Will I have to learn how to can the tomatoes? My mother used to do that, but I never helped. I was always working in the summer, trying to save money for college."

Betty laughed. "I used to do a lot of canning and freezing vegetables. But more and more the last few years, John and I just give away what we can't eat ourselves. It's our way of sharing God's love. God has given me the patience and ability to grow flowers and vegetables, so I freely give them away, just like God freely gives us his love."

"Wow! I'll bet you make a lot of people happy," Helen said.

A customer entered the coffee shop, and Helen excused herself to welcome the new person.

The pig drew lots of attention during its first week on John's desk.

"Hey, John, is that for your retirement fund?"

That was the most popular comment.

"Betty must have cut back on your allowance."

"I think I've got one of those on my desk too, it's just hidden under all my work."

"Most people have a picture of their family on their desk. Is that a relative?"

Eventually, people took time to read the words, "Prayers" and "Intercessions" and "Gratitude" on each side of the red pig. John would explain his willingness to pray for people, and usually the questioner would return later to slip a piece of paper into the pig's slot. John made it a habit to empty the porker each evening, stuffing the requests in his pocket for later perusal at his before-bed prayer time.

One night, about a week after John started the "prayer pig" project, a folded index card proclaimed the following: "Thank you, John, and praise God that your prayers for my son have been answered. He starts his new job Monday. Freida in Claims Adjusting."

Tom looked at the list of six people that, besides himself, made up the Inside-Out Project. Each was seeking to live more for others, but each in a different way. He needed to invest himself and his ministry in these people, for that is where God was investing himself. He would make time to visit them for a few minutes every week or so at their work or home, or maybe talk on the phone.

Lord, I can do this. But what happens when the number grows?

He immediately thought of Sylvia. She said she had grown her children's ministry by encouraging others. She could give him some ideas.

Tom punched her number into his cell phone.

"Hello, Tom," she answered. "I've only got a minute. What's up?

"I need some business advice. Can I take you to dinner tonight."

"No, you can't." Sylvia paused.

"No?"

"No. Mom made me promise to invite you to dinner at our house next time you called. Can you be there at six?"

"Wow. You bet! I can't pass up a home-cooked meal. I'll see you at six."

"Mom will be thrilled. 'Bye!"

A small red Ford pickup pulled into the driveway. Betty stood up amidst the hills of yellow squash and saw a young woman in jeans and a flowered blouse tentatively heading her way.

"Why, Helen! So good to see you," Betty exclaimed. "How did you know how to find me?"

Helen laughed as she gave Betty a hug. "It was kind of crazy. There's an older gentleman that comes in the coffee shop named Hank. He's always so nice. He reminds me of you and your husband. So I thought maybe he went to your church. And I was right! Isn't that wild? He knew right where you live."

Betty laughed. "Sounds like Old Dominion is making a good impression. Doesn't our pastor frequent The Wild Bird, too?"

Helen's eyes got big. "Tom Osborn? The red-haired preacher? I should have guessed that."

Betty asked, "So what brings you here today, on your day off?"

Helen didn't respond right away. She walked beside Betty's garden, looking at the vegetable plants and flowers.

"Betty," she began, "I was impressed with your giving away so much of what you grow to brighten other lives. I'd love to be a part of something like that. Will you let me help you in your garden?"

May and Chuck Beattie had constructed their home outside of Helmsville with their own hands. The twelve-hundred-square-foot white building sat on a one-acre lot, a quarter of which was garden. May always had fresh or home-canned vegetables to serve family and guests.

"Sylvia tells us your church is starting to grow," offered Chuck.

"I guess it's more pre-growth," said Tom. "We're having more in attendance, but only two have joined so far. In the United Methodist Church, membership is the number we key on."

"Oh, I know," Sylvia's dad responded. "We were Methodists all our lives, until our daughter got the job at Calvary. We joined over there to support her."

May interjected, "But taking that step to become a member is pretty important. Commitment grows a church. More squash?"

"I think Tom's got his eye on that cherry pie over on the buffet," said Sylvia.

The young pastor had to laugh. "I didn't think you saw me looking that way."

After dinner, May and Chuck insisted on clearing the table and washing dishes, so that Tom and Sylvia could visit in the den.

"I can tell that my parents like you," said Sylvia.

"Really? I was pretty sure of that, but you seem to have a gift for reading people. I think you can tell I like them a lot already."

"I could tell, and I'm glad." Sylvia's eyes twinkled as she laughed. "So what kind of business advice was it that you wanted from me? I've been wondering all day what I knew that you don't know."

He paused for a minute to formulate his words. Dishes made a muffled clatter in the kitchen.

"You know I'm trying to be a better encourager with my congregation. One segment, what we call "the Inside-Out Project," is getting especially exciting right now. I believe those six people are the key to Old Dominion's growth. I know I've mentioned them before."

"I remember," Sylvia said, twisting on the sofa to face him more directly. "You meet with them on some Sunday nights."

"I want to grow that group. It wouldn't surprise me if the size of the group doubled or tripled in a hurry."

"And you want to know how I encouraged my children's ministry parents and kids when it started to quickly expand."

"Right. You read me like a book."

"At first, there were only eight sets of parents. I would drop by their homes, chat before church, and set up group picnics. The ones I didn't see personally, I'd talk to on the phone. We bonded into a little army for God in a couple months."

Tom took a little notepad and pen from his shirt pocket. "That's where I'm at right now."

"When the group got bigger, it happened explosively. I learned to rely more on personal notes and phone calls."

"Easy enough. I've thought of that."

"But it wasn't enough."

Tom stopped writing. "It wasn't?"

"No, it wasn't. It started to wear me out. Your best tool is going to be encouraging your group to encourage others. You can't let your own limits be a limit for bringing people to God."

"Whoa. Say that again, slowly. That's priceless. Thank you, Lord."

CHAPTER 14

Ricky was starting to see how it all fit together. He started reading the Bible right after revival this year, when he finally became a Christian. Maybe all those years in the pews of Old Dominion United Methodist Church had not been wasted.

It took two weeks to read through the first time. This time he couldn't achieve that speed. Everything he read seemed to remind him of something, somewhere else in the Bible. The book just made sense!

Ricky kept a Bible commentary open on the table as he read. He wrote in a journal and in the margins of his Bible. He decided that he'd also need a marker to highlight special passages that spoke particularly to his life.

This book filled an empty place in the middle of who he was.

Lydia steered her Mercedes into a parking space and stared at the name over the door. Who in the world would name a business "Susan's Wild Bird Coffee Shop"?

It was ingenious. It was whimsical and eye-catching. Who indeed?

Lydia laughed. The answer was—Susan! She just had to go in and meet the lady.

"Good morning! I'm glad you're here," came the greeting as Lydia entered the business.

"And I'm so glad to be here," Lydia answered. "Are you Susan?"

"No, ma'am, my name is Helen. Susan, the owner, may be back later," the waitress replied. "Welcome to our coffee shop. We also have sandwiches and pastries."

"And birds! Young lady, I am impressed with the decor. This is a great marketing idea. Exactly how many of these birds are there?" Lydia said.

"Thirty," Helen answered. "When I was working on my marketing degree at Belton, this shop was used as a good example in class one day. Could I get you some coffee, say cinnamon blueberry?"

"That sounds wonderful. Thank you, Helen."

Lydia wandered around the shop, looking at all the wild birds, and then she took a seat at a small table. Two young ladies sat nearby, munching sandwiches. A bearded man with glasses sat on the far side of the room, reading a newspaper. She wondered if he might be a college professor.

When Helen brought the coffee, Lydia said, "I should introduce myself. I didn't mean to act unfriendly. I'm Lydia Michaelson."

"I'm pleased to meet you, Lydia. I'm Helen Adams," the waitress replied. "I've been working here three years, ever since I graduated from Belton. I'm hoping to save enough money to open a business of my own."

"Why, Helen, that will take a long time."

Helen blushed slightly. "I suppose it will," she said. "I'm really quite frugal, and I work six days a week. I save about half my pay."

"I wish you would take a Sunday off and come to church with me," Lydia ventured. "Life always works out better with God on your side."

"No offense intended, Lydia," she said, "but I have asked off this Sunday to try out Old Dominion United Methodist Church. I've met a lot of nice people that attend there."

"And now you've met another," Lydia answered.

"Rita!" Mandy screamed with delight, running out the kitchen door. A black BMW pulling a small rental trailer snaked its way into the driveway.

Rita Johnson emerged from the car and ran to meet her friend. Hank soon joined them in the driveway, and the three made their way to the double doors at the back of the trailer.

"I put most of my furniture in a storage unit over on Fairfax Drive. Hank, I hope this isn't too much to bring."

The trailer stretched six feet wide, seven feet high, and ten feet deep. To say it was full would be a laughable understatement.

Mandy's grandfather stood silent and expressionless, staring at Rita's belongings in the trailer. As the silence stretched toward a full minute, Rita and Mandy looked more and more worried.

"Oh, dear," Rita whispered.

"Granddaddy?" Mandy cried out, as she reached for his hand.

Suddenly it was like the sun burst forth. Hank's face broke open into a huge grin, and he began to laugh.

"Had you worried, didn't I?" Hank said triumphantly. "Rita, I said bring whatever you want, and I mean it. We are thrilled to have you as part of our household. Are you sure this is enough? C'mon, everybody, grab something and let's get this unloaded!"

Rita, of course, would have the run of the house. Her bedroom was two doors down from Mandy's room upstairs, and the room in between provided a sitting room/office space. Hank's master bedroom occupied the space next to the den downstairs.

"We saved the best bathroom just for you," Mandy proclaimed. "Let me show you!"

She grabbed Rita's hand and gently pulled her down the upstairs hall. Mandy threw the door open to an outer bathroom with two sinks and a long counter, with three light fixtures casting plentiful illumination. The inner bathroom sported a footed tub, a separate shower, and a toilet.

"Wow!" Rita exclaimed

"Okay, Rita. Repeat after me," Mandy said. "H-O-M-E."

CHAPTER 15

Crepe Myrtle Drive stretched east and west, just half a mile from the church. As far as Pastor Tom Osborn knew, no one from his church lived on this street.

At five thirty on a Monday afternoon in May, he expected most people to be at home. Tom parked his blue Avalon by the curb next to the first residence on the north side of the street and proceeded up the sidewalk.

As soon as he rang the doorbell, Tom heard a big dog start barking on the other side of the door. He discerned footsteps clicking up the hall, then, "Killer! Hush!"

Tom swallowed a lump, imagining a fierce Doberman waiting to maul him when the door opened.

Instead he was met by an overweight Irish setter, wagging its entire rear quarters as a fortyish, well-dressed brunette smiled back at him.

"Can I help you?" she said.

"Hello," said Tom. "I'm the pastor at Old Dominion United Methodist Church just down Gilbertville."

He offered his business card, and the woman opened the door to accept it, careful to keep the happy dog from nosing his way outside.

Tom continued, "I've been wanting to get to know people in the area. Have you and your family lived here long?"

Smiling, she said, "Why, that's so nice of you! I'm Mary Thomas. My husband, Frank, and I have been here four years. We've been visiting First Baptist some, but I've wondered about Old Dominion. It looks like such a homey little church."

Tom replied, "I've been pastor of the church for a little less than a year, and I really love it. I'm glad y'all have found a church home. Please know that we would welcome you, if you ever have a chance to visit. Well, I'd better move along. Nice to meet you, Mary Thomas."

"It's nice to meet you, too, Reverend," she said. "And don't let the name fool you. Killer got his name as a joke!"

Tom spent the next hour going house to house on the north side of Crepe Myrtle.

"Several weeks ago," Lydia said to the Sunday morning congregation, "I gave each of you ten dollars and asked you to bless somebody else with it. Who will tell us how they used their money?"

Several hands were immediately raised. One by one, they told of good deeds.

"I made a big casserole of macaroni and cheese for the new parents down the street," offered a gray-haired grandmother.

"I washed cars for free," a ten-year-old boy said, "but people didn't understand, and I made fifty bucks and put it in today's offering plate."

"The soup kitchen at First Baptist needed vegetables," someone else said, "so I bought ten dollars worth of green beans. They were three cans for a dollar."

A little girl tugged at Lydia's skirt.

"What is it, Jenna?" Lydia asked.

Little Jenna hugged Lydia's legs. "I got a Raggedy Ann doll for Sally, an' we played all day! Thank you, Miss Lydia!"

"And thank you all," Lydia called out. "You took my dollars much further than I could have myself. My, how you've blessed me!"

Lydia put the tape on pause. Whoever was calling caught her just in time, before she started her exercise routine.

"Hello, Lydia," said Pastor Osborn. "How is your inside-out life today?"

"Tom, I'm glad you called. That was quite a worship service yesterday morning. I don't remember much about your sermon, I'm afraid, but those testimonies about how people spent their ten dollars continue to bless me. Every time I think about it, tears come to my eyes."

Tom seemed to choke up just a little. "It really was incredible. Your little project brought a spark of life to Old Dominion."

"And to me. Learning to be generous is the best thing that's ever happened to me."

"You've discovered the key to hospitality that can transform our church. We've got to be givers of not just money or things, but everything that we are."

"Still got your golden pen, Hank?" Billy Burton asked.

Hank Walton had to laugh. "Actually, I do. But you know, Billy, I don't remember what I did to earn it. I remember that our fifth-grade teacher, Mrs. Roth, awarded it to me."

"Oh, man," Billy said, "you wrote a story about getting up and going to school. 'The toothpaste escaped its jail-like tube and ambushed my magenta toothbrush. As a team of gladiators, they were thrust into the arena, the mouth of the beast.' You don't remember writing that?"

"That was fifty-five years ago. I must have really made an impression on you."

"You just had an entertaining way of putting words together. You were the best writer in the whole school."

"And you have always been able to run a newspaper. How many copies of the Belton Courier do you sell every day?"

Billy Burton paused to do some mental arithmetic. "Let's see, I believe we're running about fifty thousand on weekdays, about twice that on Sunday."

"That's incredible. There are only a hundred thousand people in Belton. You know, I'd love to write a column like Charlie Cheese does, just about everyday life. He's really good."

Suddenly there appeared to be a twinkle in Billy's eye. "You're hired."

Hank Walton looked at his old friend. "What do you mean?"

Billy Burton straightened up in his chair. "I mean, write me a column," he said. "Send me one every Tuesday, three hundred words, I'll pay you fifty bucks. My readers will love you. How about it?"

Hank bowed his head in thought and prayer. After fifteen seconds, he raised his head and extended his hand to Billy. "I'll give it a try."

Billy gladly shook his hand. "You're a good man, Hank Walton."

CHAPTER 16

The postmaster slowly made his way to the counter. In spite of the difficulty, Mr. Miller smiled warmly at Keith.

"Hello, Keith! How's 'the book man' today?"

Keith Slappey smiled back at the friendly older gentleman. "It's been a pretty busy day. How are you? You look tired."

"Oh, I'm fine," Mr. Miller replied. "Still dragging along. What do you recommend for my next good read? What are you reading yourself?"

Keith recognized an opportunity to live inside out. What would be a book that would bring his postmaster closer to God?

Keith said, "Well, they've been out for years, but I've just discovered Frank Peretti's books. I read *This Present Darkness* and *Piercing the Darkness* last night. I think you'd really like them. I couldn't put them down."

"What are they about? I like fiction, and I always want the good guys to come out on top."

"I don't want to give too much away. They are both novels set in small towns, but are the focus of an incredible battle between good and evil, with worldwide consequences. Peretti is an incredible writer."

Keith picked up his mail and turned to leave.

Mr. Miller said, "And the good guy wins?"

As he went through the door, Keith smiled back, "You bet! God always comes out on top."

The change in the congregation at Old Dominion United Methodist Church was troublesome, but in a good way. Attendance on Sunday morning was up, from an average of sixty four months ago, to an average now of about eighty. Worship bulletins were running out; Sunday school classes were short on student books; and fellowship suppers often didn't have enough plates, cups, and plastic spoons. It surprised the congregation, and they were not able to adjust their thinking quickly enough.

For three weeks in a row, Beth Williams found her seat taken by a visitor, so she joined the choir to be sure to find a place. Tom Frankel and Andy Barnett, the ushers, found that part of the offering kept falling out of the plates, so they bought two more plates and recruited two more ushers. And the pastor asked Ricky Temple and John Carter to greet visitors, making sure they knew where to park, where the rest rooms were, and asking them to fill out a guest card.

Somehow the congregation had become contagious. They were friendlier. They were learning to live inside out.

Mrs. Miller looked at her watch. She needed to get home and start supper, but the sanctuary needed vacuuming. With all these new folks, twice a month was no longer enough.

Mrs. Miller worked at the bank, and her husband had all he could do with his job at the post office. They had always kept up Old Dominion together, she cleaning the inside and he doing the lawn and shrubbery. Lately though, her husband was troubled with a bad hip, with surgery scheduled for just after he retired in about two months.

If Mrs. Miller could just manage without him at the church, they could retire together. It was tough, but she must get it done. She wasn't going to let the Lord down.

"Hello! Anybody in here?"

She heard a voice calling from the direction of the church office, but she didn't recognize who it was.

In less than a minute, a blond young man was coming through the sanctuary door.

"You must be Mrs. Miller," he said. "I'm Keith Slappey. I thought maybe the car outside belonged to Pastor Osborn. I hoped I might borrow a book."

"No, sir, he left about an hour ago," she replied. "I'm just trying to finish cleaning the church. It takes a little more time, now that we've got more people coming. I'm proud to see them all, don't get me wrong."

Keith grinned. "I guess you could say I'm one of them," he said. "I got saved at one of the Pancake House meetings three months ago. That's when I started coming to church with my buddy, Ricky Temple."

"My, my, that boy has sure straightened himself up," she declared. "I've known Ricky his whole life, and I'd about decided he must be sleeping in church with his eyes open. He didn't seem to be catching anything, until he came to the altar during revival. Now he's a brand new man."

"I agree," Keith said. "Say, Mrs. Miller, I saw your husband at the post office this afternoon. He was moving kind of slow. Is he okay?"

"He would never tell you," she said, "but he's in a lot of pain. Supposed to have his right hip replaced when he retires in two months. But he always tries to be cheerful. I'm trying to do his part at the church right now, so he can rest at night."

"Hey!" said Keith. "Can I help? I've been praying for a way to help out at the church. You're an answer to prayer! Let me cut the grass and do the outside stuff, okay? I'll make you proud of me."

Mrs. Miller produced a huge grin, and three tears.

CHAPTER 17

Hank and Mandy had taken the Memorial Day weekend to visit Hank's brother and his family, so Rita Johnson had the big house on Maple and a pot of coffee all to herself.

Maybe, just maybe she had recovered from tax season. Even with the many extensions filed for clients, any CPA's business changed dramatically after April 15. The smaller the image of that date looked in her rearview mirror, the better the present and future appeared.

Of course, the stress of moving had been thrown into the mix this year, though that seemed minor compared to work. What a relief to get away from that condo!

Dear God, she didn't deserve this. What a house, and in a quiet neighborhood!

But really, what was she doing here? Hank would only accept a hundred dollars a month rent, which probably didn't even cover her part of the utilities, and he always had a hot breakfast and supper prepared for all of them. The 66-year-old had given no indication he was remotely interested in any kind of romance with Rita. He only said that it was nice to have a woman around the house for Mandy's sake.

Could she live here and just be a friend? That's not how American media portrayed "life in these United States." You'd have to find that in the Bible or something, "brothers and sisters in Christ."

❧

Helen Adams cradled her right hand under a large tomato, crimson with a few green streaks, and called down the row to Betty Carter, "Is this ready to pick?"

Betty turned and moved to Helen's side. Looking carefully at the red fruit, she said, "I'd pick it, for giving away. It'll last several days like that. If John and I were using it for a tomato sandwich, I'd probably wait another day or two."

"My tomato plants you gave me in the five-gallon buckets are about this far along too," Helen said. "I had a couple tomato sandwiches a couple days ago. Mmmm."

"Which brand of mayonnaise did you put on the bread?"

"Oh, should I use mayonnaise? I just made a jam sandwich. You know, slices of tomato jammed between two slices of bread."

"Some people add salt too, but try it with just mayo first."

"When I start my business," Helen said in a kind of trance, "I think I'll grow tomatoes and geraniums in pots in the window."

Betty smiled at her. "What other ideas do you have? What will you sell?"

"If I can get a place near the college, I'd like to sell gently used furniture, lots of book shelves, lamps, just generally things a college student might decorate with," she said. "I think, with the right kind of advertising, my store could appeal to young married couples too, and maybe people that want to inexpensively furnish a garage apartment or a cabin."

"I'll bet you could make it work. Don't you want to sell coffee, too?"

"The problem with that, is I'd be competing against my present boss. I couldn't do that. She's been too good to me."

"Why, that's a sweet thought!" Betty said.

The bar was hopping tonight. In Ricky's opinion, there was no better place to watch the NBA finals.

His old friend Ben Williams had had a few beers too many. The ball game no longer held his attention, and he turned his attention to Ricky.

"Ya know, you might close down this place, Rick," Ben said. "Freddy's Sports Bar makes its profit on beer. Watcha have, just one beer tonight? Or was it one?"

Ricky smiled and said, "You know, old boy, these soft drinks I'm buying make a whole lot more money for Freddy's than that Bud you're drinking."

With a monstrous dunk on the TV screen, the crowd in the bar erupted. Ben looked up, wondering what the commotion was.

"Rick," he said, "nothing upsets you any more. And you grin a lot. That's all right. How do ya do that, without another beer?"

Ricky's wheels started to turn. Was this an opportunity to help Ben straighten up a little?

"I get a lot of tips out of the Bible," Ricky said. "It's strange stuff sometimes, but it works. Like, 'Don't worry about if you'll have enough food or clothing tomorrow. Look at how God takes care of the birds and animals. You know he cares even more for people.'"

"Yeah, but if you can't do nothin' else, you gotta at least worry, or you ain't doin' nothing at all."

"You would be amazed how much better life is when you don't sweat the small stuff."

"Hey," Ben said, "sometime when you're reading your Bible, write me down a few of those life-changing little things. I might give 'em a try."

"Be glad to, pal," he answered. "Whoa! Did you see that shot? It was just about half court! Nothing but net!"

CHAPTER 18

Nobody could make meat loaf like Hank Walton. He only used ground sirloin and added just the right amount of horseradish.

"Granddaddy," Mandy said, "can we have the rest of the meat loaf for breakfast tomorrow?"

Rita and Hank laughed.

"Meat loaf is not for breakfast, Mimi," Rita replied. After a pause, she added, "Let's just finish it now!"

"Okay, you two," Hank said. "You've stuffed yourselves already. The meat loaf will be a side dish for us tomorrow night. That way, Rita won't have to make anything else spectacular."

As they finished supper, Rita asked Mandy, "Still working on your homework?"

"I've just got a little more reading in science," she said.

"If you'll go ahead and finish that, we can play a game or two of Scrabble."

"Okay. I'll be back in twenty minutes," Mandy said as she headed for her room.

Hank began clearing the table, as Rita ran dish water in the sink.

"Looks like I need to run the dishwasher tonight," she said. "Are you going to join us for Scrabble?"

"I think I'd like to work on my newspaper column, if you don't mind," he replied. "I'm glad it's your turn to do dishes." Hank took a quick glance at the printed schedule on the side of the refrigerator to be sure.

"I would be glad to volunteer myself for cooking more than two nights a week," she added, "but I'm a little inexperienced. When you live alone, it's easy to just open a can of soup or a cup of yogurt."

Hank smiled. "I've got an idea," he said. "I want to teach Mandy to cook a little. Maybe we could all cook together once a week."

"That's great," Rita replied. "Mandy has already figured out I'm not a world-famous chef."

Hank sat down at the kitchen table, sipping a cup of decaf coffee. "We like you just the way God made you. We're glad you're here."

Rita washed pots and pans without speaking for a minute, while the dishwasher hummed.

"Hank," she said, "this is a great house, and you and Mandy have been really good to me. I feel a little guilty about feeling comfortable."

Concern clouded Hank's face. He said, "I know our household is unconventional, and sometimes I wonder what your friends think, or what neighbors think. Rita, I've been as honest with you as I know how to be. I invited you to live with us because God nudged me in that direction. He knows I need help with Mandy. I don't want her to turn out like me. I want her to grow into a young woman. I don't expect you to be her mother or grandmother. Just continue being the Christian woman you already are."

Rita continued washing dishes, obviously deep in thought. In another minute, she rinsed the last pan and drained out the water.

Rita said, "I just need to tell you that, if you ever feel uncomfortable with my being here, let me know, and I'll find another place. I'll understand."

Hank smiled. "Fair enough," he said. "Honesty is basic."

Tom punched one number. He now had Sylvia Beattie on speed dial.

"I'm glad you called, Tom. It's been two days since we've talked."

"It's been a busy week. I'm sorry. Look, I know it's Saturday night, but…is there any chance you could take time off from Calvary Baptist to attend Old Dominion in the morning?"

"I guess you're right about my ability to read people. I was planning on coming. It just felt like a good time."

"That's amazing. God is so good."

"It wouldn't hurt for your congregation to know you've got a girlfriend, Tom."

Old Dominion Church was bubbling with a sense of anticipation today, for two reasons. First, a porcelain pitcher and wash basin sat on a small table near the altar rail. Was this to be one of Pastor Osborn's sermon 'visual aids'? And second, the first line after the prelude in the Sunday bulletin read, "Reception of New

Members." There were many guesses as to who that might be.

When the prelude ended, Tom Osborn stepped behind the pulpit. "As many of you remember," he began, "I've been teaching a confirmation class for three of our young people this month. Today, they and a few others will be joining our church.

"One of the things they learned is that, in the United Methodist Church, you can be baptized in one of three ways. We're all familiar with sprinkling baptism, which uses drops of water on the head of the one being baptized. I think you are also familiar with baptism by immersion, which we would probably do in a swimming pool, or maybe in the baptistry over at Sharon Baptist. But we don't hear much about the third option, which is baptism by pouring. We'll see that today.

"I invite those who have decided to join the church today to come forward at this time."

The three youths in the front pew popped up and came forward. Keith Slappey, with a wide smile, also came up. He would be baptized by pouring, using the pitcher and basin. Helen Adams quietly made her way to the front, from her seat near the back where she had been sitting with Susan, the owner of the coffee shop, a first-time visitor.

"Please turn to page thirty-five in your hymnal, for our baptism and membership service," Pastor Osborn continued.

"I remind you that the United Methodist Church honors baptism done at other churches. If there are others who feel God calling them to join this church today, feel free to come forward now."

A family of four sat halfway back on the left side. There were a few exchanged glances and words amongst them, then they also came to the front.

The red-haired lady near the middle of the church could tell that Tom was surprised, and started praying silently.

Only three people had joined Old Dominion Church in the last three years.

CHAPTER 19

After church, Lydia carefully maneuvered herself to the back of the clump, congratulating Helen for joining today.

"I'd love to take you to lunch, if you don't have other plans," she offered to Helen. "I'm so glad you chose to be part of our church."

"The only plans I had," Helen Adams said, "were to heat up last night's leftovers. They'll wait."

"Well, then, let's go to the college," Lydia said. "They do a fine Sunday lunch."

"I remember," said Helen. "It's strategic, since that's when they know they'll have people from the community eating there."

After they were seated with their meal in the cafeteria, Lydia gave thanks for the food and Helen's church membership.

"I used to wonder, as a student," Helen said, "why the town folks always sat away from us. I think I know now. It's a little loud."

"If the church hopes to attract any of these young adults, they will have to welcome the noise. It just seems full of life, to me."

"I used to spend a lot of time at that little coffee shop across the street. You may not remember it. It's closed now."

For a few minutes, they ate salad and listened to the chatter of college kids.

"Helen, I bought that old coffee shop a couple weeks ago," Lydia said. "It looked like a good investment."

Helen's eyes brightened. "I think you're right. With the right management, that would be a great location."

Lydia Michaelson sat up a little straighter in her chair. "Helen, that's where you fit in. If you've got a good concept in mind, I'll be your financial backer. I'd like to see a successful business in that building."

Keith recognized the new customer entering The Book House. "Great to have you, Pastor," he called out. "Let me know if I can help you."

Tom browsed for fifteen or twenty minutes, then made his way to the counter with a dozen used books.

"This is quite a place, Keith. I wish I'd stopped in here before now."

"The owners really know good books," he replied. "They like to travel around the country, and they've made a lot of connections with book wholesalers and other book stores."

Keith began to ring up Tom's purchases. "This may sound irreverent, but I'm having a blast being a Christian. I never knew what I was missing"

"I heard you were starting to help with cleaning the church. Mrs. Miller says you're a Godsend."

"I want to take the job over when she and her husband retire, if that's okay with the church. As a volunteer, of course."

"That sounds great, Keith, but it can be a mighty big job. I think it's too much for one man."

Keith looked disappointed. He tried to think of something to say to change his pastor's mind.

Tom continued, "I've often wondered if that job could be done by a group of volunteers, with maybe one person in charge as coordinator."

Keith's face brightened. "I could do that! I would love to give new people a chance to get involved, hands-on."

"Consider it done, then. I'll talk to the Trustees. I suspect they'll be easily convinced. And may God continue to bless you."

The pastor parked his blue Toyota Avalon a few yards up the curb on the north side of Boxwood Drive. Tom had a few flyers in his hand, advertising what Old Dominion church had to offer. Sometimes visiting seemed easier with something to hand out.

The first house on the right was two-story and in need of a fresh coat of paint. He tried the doorbell a couple of times, with no response. He rapped sharply on the door and immediately heard movement inside.

An elderly woman opened the door with considerable effort. She smiled brightly and said, "Yes?"

The slight, white-haired lady wore an old dress covered by a faded apron. Her blue bedroom slippers looked comfortably worn in.

"Good afternoon," Tom Osborn said. "I'm out trying to meet people in the neighborhood. I'm the pastor at Old Dominion United Methodist Church, just down Gilbertville." Tom reached out with a brochure. "This looks like a great neighborhood to live in."

Accepting the pamphlet, she said, "Nice to meet you, Brother Osborn. I'm Mary Eddy. Yes, I've lived here for sixty-two years since I married my late husband, Tom Osborn Eddy. At that time, this was the only house on the street. I remember when your little church was built."

"Wow, Mrs. Eddy," he said, "that's amazing that your husband's first and middle names were the same as my first and last names. Of course, we're probably not related. I was raised in the Midwest. Have you ever been to our church?"

"No," she said. "I used to go to the First Christian Church some, but it's been many years. I sold my old car last year, and Community Transit doesn't run on Sundays."

"Mrs. Eddy, would you come to my church this Sunday if I have somebody pick you up before Sunday school, say 9:45 a.m.?"

Mary Eddy started to laugh, in a way that could only be described as a cackle. "My goodness, Brother Tom Osborn. This is a bit unexpected," she said. "Yes, I'll be ready. I'm honored to be invited."

"Thank you so much." Tom beamed. "Can I say a prayer for you before I go?"

Rita could hear Hank's steady taps on the keyboard of his office computer in the next room. She sat on the sofa, trying to read a John Grisham novel.

An occasional giggle floated down the stairwell from Mandy's room. Hank's granddaughter had weekend company, and Rita was feeling like a spare tire.

She considered climbing the stairs, to ask if she could join Mandy and Lisa. No, she was too mature for that. Maybe she could offer to take them bowling or watch a movie.

Rita decided that she had to allow Mandy to have other friends. She needed girlfriends her own age.

Rita went back to her novel, but she just could not concentrate. After a few minutes, she closed the novel and laid it down.

She opened her cell phone to the list of contacts. Brandi Porter was a member of the same gym as Rita, and they often chatted as they walked on adjacent treadmills. Maybe she'd like to go see a movie.

CHAPTER 20

"Brother Tom," Ricky said, "I've got a friend that wants help understanding what the Bible teaches. I didn't think I'd ever get Ben in church, but I'm thinking his curiosity might give me a chance to lead him to Christ."

Ricky Temple had stopped by Tom Osborn's office early on Monday morning, hoping to catch him before anyone else did.

"Well," Tom said, "I've got several books that might be a good starting point for him."

Ricky frowned.

"I'm afraid that won't do for Ben," he said. "He does so much reading at work, he doesn't want anything deeper than a birthday card in his leisure hours. I thought maybe you could come down to the bar and lead a short weekly discussion. I could get five or six other people to come."

Reverend Osborn rubbed his chin a few times, trying to encourage rational thought. The preacher in a bar? He would probably scare as many prospects away as Ricky could attract.

After a minute, Tom said, "You know, you might be able to reach folks in the bar better than I could. No offense, Ricky, but the people you want to reach have more in common with you than they do me. You know enough to lead the kind of group you're talking about."

"Me?" Ricky replied. "I don't know."

"Tell you what," Tom said. "Stop and see me a day or two before your group meets each week, and you and I will talk about what your topic will be. I'll give you my ideas, and you take it from there."

"Brother Tom, I might be able to do it that way. Would it bother you if I prayed about it first?"

Susan sat down at the small table, across from the red-haired pastor. The usual bagel and coffee crowded in next to his open laptop.

"Did you know," she started, "that we now close from 10 a.m. to one on Sundays? Helen is in charge of the Wild Bird when I'm not here, and since we both want to attend your church on Sundays, I decided we would just lock the doors and go to Old Dominion."

Tom Osborn smiled. "I guess you're making quite a sacrifice. I appreciate it."

Susan laughed. "Those were just break-even hours, anyway. That little business barely paid the waitress. Tell me about the Pancake House meetings you just cancelled."

"We had been getting together after church on Sunday nights, every other week," he replied, "to talk about how to live inside out. Lately, practically everyone that came to Sunday night church was also going to the meeting afterward, so it made sense just to combine the two. I preach, then we have some cookies and brownies, and then we share our experiences of how we try to live inside out."

Susan paused for a moment to gather her thoughts.

"Tom, you've really made an impact at the Wild Bird Coffee Shop. Since Helen became a Christian, and I started attending worship again for the first time in years, everything seems to be running smoothly in here. Business has even picked up, I don't know why. I think it's time you took your business elsewhere."

The pastor laughed and laughed, until tears started running down his face. Susan only smiled.

"Tom," she said, "I'm serious."

He stared at her, the smile fading from his face. "What do you mean? I don't get it."

Susan reached out to grasp his hand.

"You have such a knack at getting to know people," she said. "God uses that. I know that wherever you are a regular customer, people will see Jesus. I can serve him best by sending you someplace else. So Tom, for the love of God, find some place else to have bagels and coffee. Okay?"

Ralph rubbed people the wrong way at Edison Fund Insurance Company. John Carter did his best to love him like Jesus did, but it seemed like an uphill battle.

"Well, John," Ralph said, "how's the pig man?"

"It's a great day," John replied. "God has really blessed me."

"Is that so?" asked the underwriter. "It's probably just luck. Say, how does this magic pig work? Just put a dollar in the slot and you get your wish?"

"No charge, Ralph," John replied. "I pray for any requests that are put in the slot, on my own time."

Ralph smirked and said, "Sounds like a waste of time. You must need to make some new friends."

"I'm convinced that God hears every prayer. There have been some incredible results."

Ralph smiled and stared at the red pig on John's desk.

"Prayers, intercessions, gratitude," he read aloud. As Ralph turned to walk away, he added, "I wonder if our beloved Mr. Edison would approve of such a blatant religious display in the workplace. You might give it a thought."

CHAPTER 21

Betty Carter noticed that her lunch companion's yellow T-shirt was drawing attention in the Belton College cafeteria. She was pleased.

A tall, gray-bearded man stopped by, lunch tray in hand. "Helen Adams! Why, it's great to see you. How are you?"

"Fine, Dr. Jones. Please meet my friend, Betty Carter. Won't you join us?"

Ed Jones, professor of marketing at the college, put down his tray and borrowed a chair from the next table.

"All right," he said, "you've got me curious. What does your T-shirt mean by 'Coming Soon. Just What You Need'?"

Helen grinned. "See, I was listening in your classes. I'm opening a shop soon, in the old coffee shop building, and I'm calling it Just What You Need. We're enjoying a great lunch, but I'm also doing a bit of advertising."

"What will you sell?"

Helen turned to a stack of yellow fliers between her and Betty, and passed one to her former teacher.

"I hope to have just what every college student needs," Helen replied. "Bookshelves, rugs, lamps, all secondhand but in good shape. I want to keep copy paper and printer ink cartridges too, as well as pens and other school supplies. I'll have some posters and art prints. Of course, I'll need to carry a wide assortment of snacks, and a wide variety of ramen noodles."

Betty said, "Professor, do you remember Helen's pickup truck that's the same color as her shirt?"

Dr. Jones quickly replied, "Betty, when Helen was a student here, she drove a red pickup."

Helen pointed out the cafeteria window to the parking lot and said, "Not anymore."

Sipping on a cold bottle of water, Mr. Miller sat in a lawn chair and watched carefully as Keith Slappey trimmed shrubbery.

"What about these big shoots, sir?" Keith asked. "They're going to leave a big stub showing."

Mr. Miller peered carefully at the shrub. "If you'll cut those big shoots a foot or so shorter, the stubs will be hidden inside the shrub. You're doing a great job, Keith. I'm sorry I let the church shrubbery go so long without trimming, but I just can't stand very long with this bad hip."

"Hey, it's a blessing to me, Mr. Miller. I'm thrilled with the new life God gave me. I just want to serve in his church any way I can."

"Good night, Granddaddy," Mandy said as she gave Hank a long hug. "I'm going to my room. Tell Rita goodnight for me when she gets home."

"Goodnight, angel," he replied. "Remember we're all going to the Pancake House for breakfast before church."

"I remember," she said, as she headed for the stairs. "I already know I want waffles."

"Sounds good to me. See you in the morning."

Hank Walton leaned back in his desk chair. His newspaper column was not due in Billy's office at the Courier until Tuesday morning, but he always did his best to finish a first draft before Monday.

This would be his fourth column. The first had been a general introduction of himself and about the editor's invitation to him to write a column. The second column had been about his first dog, Denny. Last week's column was a short piece of fiction that imagined an outer space visitor's trip to one of Earth's fast-food restaurants. He determined that this column would address living inside out.

> A curious thing happened at Norman's Foodliner last Thursday. Some would argue that odd things happen at Norman's all the time. This one I was a witness to.
>
> It was a little after five, and three cashiers had all they could do to keep up with the after-work crowd. Every line had at least seven customers, many with shopping carts fully loaded.
>
> People were getting impatient. A baby was crying. Grumblings were passing from customer to customer, and line to line. I did my best not to pass the grumble in my line on to the next

person, but it jumped over me like a forest fire jumps a small creek.

In line one, a father with a teenage son abruptly steered their cart out of the queue and parked it to the side. The dad said a few words to the boy and pointed to the bagging station at the end of line one, while he himself began bagging groceries in line two.

I saw the harried cashier turn her head to say, "Thank you!" and then continue on at her frantic pace.

Why did they give up their place in line to voluntarily help paid employees? What would those folks waiting at home for them think, watching the clock and trying to keep supper warm?

I watched for a half a minute, no more. It was all I could stand. I pulled my shopping cart out of line and pitched in to help.

The lines moved more quickly now. People started smiling. And wonder of wonders, the baby even stopped crying. In just a couple of minutes, the cashiers had caught up, and the customers were heading for their cars or their suburban three-bedroom-with-a-bath-and-a-half homes.

Hank decided to take a break and finish his column later, explaining how people that lived for others made lives more bearable.

CHAPTER 22

It was Saturday night, and John was still thinking about Friday morning.

Everybody knew Eva. In the beginning years of Edison Fund Insurance Company, she had worked side by side with her husband, selling and writing policies, and studying to become an expert on government regulations for the insurance industry. She eased out of the everyday affairs of the business when the twins were born, but she still came by as often as she could. This was her "other baby."

When John Carter arrived at work Friday morning, Mrs. Edison was standing at his desk. She had his "prayer pig" in her hands, turning it slowly from side to side.

He felt his stomach start to knot up. He had meant to remove most of the letters of "Prayers, Intercession, Gratitude" and just leave "PIG," but he hadn't gotten around to it yet. This could be trouble.

"Good morning, John," Eva Edison said. "I had not noticed your pig before. I had one just like this as a child, except that mine was for coins. You've transformed it into a symbol of your faith."

John swallowed and forced himself to smile wider than he thought his fear would allow.

"Yes, ma'am," he replied. "It's my way of contributing a little extra to the company."

She sat the pig back in its place. Glancing around his desktop, she spied a small notepad, tore off a sheet, and then quickly wrote a few words. She folded the paper in half and deposited it into the pig.

"Thank you, John," Eva said. "You're a good man."

A back room at Freddy's sported a paper sign, "High Life, Saturday, 9 p.m."

"I'm starting to get a handle on my life a little bit," Ricky Temple began. "I didn't realize it, but some of you had been a little worried about me. I appreciate y'all.

"It's got a lot to do with church, or the Bible anyway. That's why I wanted to get this group together. Since you care about me, it's only fair that I share the good stuff."

Ricky shifted in his chair a little, and looked around at the other six people in the small side room at Freddy's Sports Pub. All but two he had known since junior high, and all were regular Saturday night pub customers.

"I hope you're gonna translate for us," Dorothy said. "I know the Bible has some good guidelines. I can tell by how my parents live. But when I start reading thees and thous and begats, I just close it up and lay it down."

Ben strode into the room, beer in hand. "The sign on the door said 'High Life,' so I brought one with me. Sorry I'm late. Had to see a man about a dog."

He sat in one of the two empty chairs in the circle.

"I think everybody's here now," Ricky said. "I'm going to start with the two Bible verses that made the most difference to me.

"One is the very first in the Bible, 'In the beginning, God created the heavens and the earth.' Now, I can't prove that, because I wasn't around when he did it. But if I don't give God the benefit of the doubt on that, it's going to be hard to accept the rest of his wisdom in the Bible."

"How do you know God is a he?" Janet asked. "Does God have male body parts?"

Laughter erupted around the room.

"Get your mind out of the gutter," Ben said. "This is a Bible study!"

With a smirk on his face, Andy said in a stilted voice, "Oh, let us not chase hither and yon after lower subjects."

Ricky said, "Actually, Janet, God has all the best female and male qualities. But Jesus called him 'Father,' so I go with the male pronouns."

Ricky grabbed his Bible and turned to a page near the back. "This is the second verse that was the key for me: 'All Scripture is useful for teaching and helping people and for correcting them and showing them how to live.' That's in the second book of Timothy."

"I missed it," Andy said. "Explain what that means for me."

"It tells me," Ricky said, "that the Bible is for helping us find a better life. Man, before I discovered that, I thought God was like some holy policeman, trying to catch me breaking some rule."

~

Later that night, over on Maple Street, Hank Walton slid into bed and turned out the lamp on the table.

His newspaper column was finished for next week, earlier than usual.

He heard a car pull up in the driveway. "Must be Rita's date, bringing her home," he mumbled. "Seemed like a nice guy." He drifted off to sleep.

Some time later, Hank was awakened by a sharp noise, something like a slap. He listened carefully, trying to make some sense out of what he heard.

A male voice chuckled, from the direction of the den.

Rita's voice was next, but it sounded stressed, even angry.

Hank jumped out of bed and quickly donned his robe. He opened the door from his room, more quickly than he intended, and it slammed against the doorstop.

"Everything all right out here?" he called out to Rita in the den.

The man who had been Rita's date jumped up and looked in Hank's general direction, obviously surprised.

"Frank was just leaving," Rita said, her voice as taut as piano wire.

Her date quickly exited the kitchen door. Rita gave the door an angry kick.

CHAPTER 23

"At last," Susan said. The last client had just exited Susan's Wild Bird Coffee Shop. "Helen, I dearly love our customers, don't get me wrong. But I'm eager to hear how plans for your shop are coming along."

Helen Adams sat in the chair across from her employer and tossed the Belton Courier onto the next table.

"Let me tell you, Susan," she started, "my landlord can get things done! Lydia and I talked just yesterday about colors for the three rooms of the building, and she's got a painter lined up to start next Monday. But I'm still a little worried about cash flow. It doesn't seem like I've got enough to attract daily or weekly customers. I want to be able to pay the bills."

Susan quietly sipped coffee for a dozen seconds, and then responded, "I've always depended on coffee sales to pay the bills. Have you got room for a coffee corner?"

Helen said, "Susan, I made the decision not to sell coffee. I don't want to cut in to your business. You've been too good to me."

Susan smiled and replied, "We don't get much business from the college. Maybe a professor or two. They usually get one cup of coffee, then take up space in here for an hour."

Helen stared out the window. "I don't know. I still think I might feel a little guilty."

"Tell you what," Susan said, "I've got something I want you to consider. These birds are just part of a large collection. For fifty dollars a month, I'll let you rent thirty jungle birds, you call the coffee area in your business Susan's Wild Bird Coffee Shop II, and you buy all your supplies through me."

⤳

"How is your blended family developing?" asked Tom. "I saw the three of you sitting in three different parts of the church this morning. Everything okay?"

Hank spoke warmly into the phone, "Couldn't be better, Tom. Rita is a good influence for Mandy, without monopolizing her friendship. She seems to accept me as kind of a father figure. I'm glad Rita doesn't feel compelled to always hang around with us."

"Do you think she's resolved to always be single? I caught myself wondering the other day how it would affect Mandy if Rita were to marry and move out."

Hank paused to consider the question. "I really don't know about that. Rita still has an occasional date, but most of the time she's happy to be a homebody. I'll have to get back to you on that."

"Hank, I'm really enjoying your newspaper columns. I don't have to ask you about inside-out living, since reports of it seem to find their way into your writing. Keep up the good work."

❧

Tom grabbed another brownie and headed for the front of the church. He pulled a folding chair to the center and sat down.

"Okay, everybody," he said. "Let's come back now. Time to talk about our week of inside-out living."

The two or three conversation clusters at the back disassembled and joined the rest of the thirty-five already seated.

"Brother Tom," an older man said on his right, "are you still going out visiting on Mondays?"

"Fred," the pastor replied, "I've switched to Thursdays. People seemed to be losing their resolve to visit us when I visited too long before a Sunday. How about you? Are you and Mildred still making your rounds?"

"Yessir, nearly every week," Fred replied, "and we've discovered that something in hand helps bring a positive response."

The pastor replied, "Do you mean folks like our colorful brochures?"

Chuckles could be heard here and there throughout the gathered flock. Tom wondered what was humorous.

Someone called out, "It's not the brochures, Preacher. It's Mildred's strawberry pies!"

Tom Osborn had to laugh at himself. "Well, judging by the number of visitors you've brought with you lately, those are tremendous pies!"

Spontaneous applause erupted.

Fred stood up and looked around, asking, "Anybody else got an idea for gifts? Sometimes my wife hasn't got time to bake, and visit too." Mildred nodded in agreement.

"We carry our neighbors fresh loaves of bread from the freezer," Catherine Bubber said. "Every once in a while, I do schedule a bread day, wherein I make a dozen loaves. Pans of yeast rolls make a big impression too."

"How else are y'all living inside out?" Tom asked. He loved to use that word *y'all*. He wondered how the rest of the country got by without it.

Maxine raised her hand. "Preacher," she began, "My grandson, Tanner, mowed the tiny lawn of the elderly lady next door a couple of weeks ago. Well, I pointed out to him several other senior citizens within a block of my house that struggled to keep their yards cut. Guess what? Yesterday, he and his whole football team descended on our area with mowers and string trimmers, and they mowed every one of those lawns I had pointed out. Took them less than an hour. And they gave each homeowner one of our nifty, colorful, informative brochures, so they'd know it was a God thing."

"Good job!" Tom exclaimed. "By the way, these are the best brownies I've ever had."

"Mr. Morris," Sarah said, as she stuck her head in his office door, "Lydia Michaelson would like a few minutes with you, if possible."

Franklin Morris took a quick look at his desk calendar. "Looks like I have an open morning. When would she like to come in?"

"Actually, sir, she's here right now."

"Oh!" he said in surprise. "Well, send her in."

In a moment, Lydia had entered the office of her financial advisor. It always amazed him that she was in her eighties, but she didn't look a day over sixty-five. "Good morning, Franklin."

"Good morning, dear friend," he replied. "How can I help you?"

"You've been encouraging me to help other people with my money," she said, "and praise God, I've been doing just that. I find it's incredibly fulfilling."

Franklin replied, "God promises to bless those who are able to give to others. You're proving that to be true."

"Yes, I am," she replied. "But could I do it to the tune of two million dollars?"

CHAPTER 24

As Keith Slappey jumped out of the car, he called out, "Good Sunday morning, Mrs. Eddy."

The small eighty-year-old stood at the end of her sidewalk.

"Good morning, Keith," she replied. "I'm looking forward to seeing my new friends at Old Dominion."

Keith opened the passenger side door of his black 2005 Ford Mustang and offered his hand for support as she carefully got into the front seat.

After closing her door, Keith glanced at Mrs. Eddy's house. The two-story residence sat on about a quarter-acre lot. Its blue paint was faded to near white and was peeling badly. Otherwise, the structure looked pretty sound.

Entering the car, Keith ventured, "Mrs. Eddy, you've got a great house. If you had it to do over, would you have your house painted blue, or some other color?"

"I really loved the blue when it was first painted," she replied, "but when it started to fade, I thought white would have been a better choice."

Keith said, "Now that all the houses nearby are plain old brick, I'll bet a white house on the corner would be gorgeous."

"I believe you're right," Mrs. Eddy said.

Keith vowed that he would make it happen.

John's "prayer pig" ministry had blessed him and many other people. God often answered in miraculous ways when John prayed persistently for the requests his coworkers entrusted to him.

He watched with great curiosity from the break room at Edison Fund Insurance that morning. Ralph Edwards was walking toward John's desk with a piece of paper in his hand. He looked around, as if afraid that someone would see him, and quickly inserted the paper into the pig's slot. Ralph wasted no time in leaving the area.

A month ago, Ralph was criticizing John for this "blatant religious display." Could it be that Ralph was actually asking for a prayer?

KJ's Cafe had started carrying bagels especially for the red-headed preacher. The coffee was very good, though there were only two varieties.

"Those things any good?" a balding trucker asked, as he pulled up a chair at Tom's table.

"Ah, it's just bread," Tom said. "Kind of dense. I guess I got in the habit of eating the same old thing every day."

"I know what you mean. I always get two sausage biscuits and a red apple. I don't want to have to make any major decisions this early. Hey, I'm Buddy Cooper."

The trucker extended his hand, and Old Dominion's pastor shook it firmly. Buddy Cooper looked strong enough to wrestle alligators.

"I'm Tom Osborn. I've been coming to KJ's about a month now. I got kicked out of the last place I was getting breakfast."

Buddy stared at Tom a second, and then ventured, "Get in a fight? Some folks are ornery, early in the morning."

Tom laughed. "No, nothing like that. I'm a Methodist pastor, and the owner said, since I already got her and her main waitress going to my church, I'd be wasting my time to keep going there. I needed to eat someplace else and keep building up the church."

Buddy Cooper grinned and had a hearty laugh at Tom's expense. "You'll have to excuse my prejudice. With your red hair, I thought maybe you had a bad temper. Man, that beats all. I've never heard of a preacher getting kicked out of a restaurant."

"It did shock me at first, but I guess I can see her point."

The two men ate and drank coffee for a minute.

Buddy spoke first. "I used to go to church, back when I was married. June died seven years ago, breast cancer. I started driving long haul for a few years, to get my mind squared away. I guess I got out of the church habit."

Tom drank a few sips of coffee.

"That's rough, Buddy. How long were you married?"

"June died on our tenth anniversary, February 14. It was kind of romantic, in a weird kind of way. She made me promise to always make Valentine's Day special."

"So you wouldn't spend the day feeling sorry for yourself?"

"Yeah, that's it. Now, every February 14, I buy a red rose for every teacher in the elementary school near my house, every secretary, every lady that works there. They look forward to it."

"That's what I call keeping the love alive. That's amazing."

Buddy and Tom continued eating. When Tom had half a bagel left and Buddy had one sausage biscuit left, Tom said, "Buddy, you still love God, don't you?"

"I guess I never stopped," the trucker replied.

Tom pushed his half bagel over to Buddy, and pulled Buddy's sausage biscuit toward himself. The trucker watched him carefully.

Tom said, "Time to break a habit, all right? You try a bagel, I'll try your biscuit. How about coming to Old Dominion United Methodist Church this Sunday?"

CHAPTER 25

Mondays were Ricky's day off from the sporting goods department at Bestmart. He had a standing appointment with his pastor, every other Monday at 9 a.m.

"Tell me how your 'High Life' Bible study is going," Tom Osborn said. "Still having about six people?"

"Yeah, give or take one or two," Ricky answered. "We meet for about thirty minutes. Last week, when we talked about the crucifixion, they stayed around for nearly an hour."

"Do you feel like they take it seriously?"

"Mostly. Ben Williams, my oldest buddy, is one I really wanted to reach, but he always seems to have a couple beers in him when we meet."

"He's probably hearing more than you think. I remember, when I was drinking at the frat pretty regular at college, a couple beers didn't dull me up that much."

"You may be right. Brother Tom, we'll be talking about salvation this week. I'm not sure what to expect. All they really need to do is believe that Jesus died for them. Am I right?"

"Basically. But they've got to believe *in* Jesus, not just about him. That's what we call repentance."

Ricky seemed a little perplexed. He said, "They have to feel sad and guilty?"

"No, to repent means to turn in the direction of following Jesus. For some folks, it's a really wrenching experience, when they realize how far they've got to change direction. And some people have been going in generally the right direction, but have never committed to Jesus."

"I think one or two are about ready to take that step," Ricky said. "I hope I don't mess it up."

"You won't. Your own salvation experience will help you."

❧

"You've quit, looks like to me," Hank said.

"Quit what?" Rita replied.

"Quit dating. You haven't been out in a month."

"How do you know? For all you know, I may be meeting some guy for lunch every day."

"Are you?" Hank quickly shot back.

"No. But I could have been," Rita snapped.

Rita was taking her regular turn of washing dishes. Hank was sipping his after-dinner decaf coffee.

After another minute, Hank ventured, "Maybe you're fishing in the wrong pond. The over-aggressive guy I scared off a few weeks ago is probably rare."

Rita replied, just above a mumble, "I must be special. I get them all."

He sipped. She washed. Two minutes went by.

"What would be the top quality on your wish list?"

Pondering his question, she finally answered, "He needs to be a Christian. A real one. His life has to say it, not his mouth."

"Great!" Hank said. "Are you looking in Christian places?"

"Well, the last two were accountants, and the one before that was a pharmacist. You don't get more respectable than that."

"Were they Christians?"

"I really don't know if they ever went to church. But they seemed nice enough. And they were kind enough to ask me out."

"Rita, you don't have to be desperate," Hank said. "Pray for God to send you a decent Christian man. In the meantime, you know that you've got me and Mandy."

"I wonder if they've got more to choose from in Minnesota, where my parents moved to last year."

"Pray first," Hank advised. "God will make sure you're in the right place at the right time."

Betty carried a basket of large, exquisitely ripe tomatoes in her right hand. A few brochures describing activities at Old Dominion Church were tucked into the side of the basket.

Though these apartments were little more than a block from Betty and John's home, she had never ventured to visit here before.

Betty rang the doorbell with her left hand. Five seconds later, a teenage boy answered the door and stood staring at Betty.

"Hello, I'm Betty Carter. John and I live over on Pine Street. Could I speak to your parents, please?"

"Mom," he shouted, "somebody at the door!"

The young man and Betty stood in silence, waiting for his mother to arrive. He snuck an appreciative look at the tomatoes.

It occurred to him that he could probably make two tasty, juicy sandwiches out of any one of the tomatoes in Mrs. Carter's basket. He was also reminded that, as of then, he had not yet had a tomato sandwich that year.

The young man's mother arrived, and Betty introduced herself again.

"I'm Fran Smith," the lady of the house said, "and I guess you've met Frankie."

"I'm pleased to meet you both," Betty said.

Betty reached into the basket. Frankie's taste buds started to dance.

She extracted a church brochure from the tomato basket and said, "Fran, I'd be honored if you and Frankie and the family would come visit us this Sunday at Old Dominion United Methodist Church. If you don't already have a church home, that is."

Frankie eagerly answered, "We need a church, don't we, Mom? It's just the two of us, and we'll be there this Sunday!"

Fran's mouth dropped open, as she stared at her son. "Um, well, okay," she managed.

"Oh, and by the way," Betty Carter added, "would you like some tomatoes? We have more than we know what to do with."

CHAPTER 26

Arnold Miller was determined to be a good patient. Sure, the postmaster's old hip had been painful for a few months, but today's operation promised to take care of that. His job today was to serve the Lord somehow from his hospital bed.

"Good morning," the nurse greeted. "I'm Sharon. I'll be in the operating room with Doctor Tangle for your surgery. Please tell me your full name and date of birth."

"Good morning, Sharon! Glad to meet you," he answered. "I'm Arnold Andrew Miller, born February 19 in 1945. This is my wife, Jolene, and our friend, Keith Slappey."

Sharon glanced at the two persons sitting on the other side of the bed. "Nice to meet you two. We'll take good care of Mr. Miller today."

"Arnold," Mr. Miller said. "Please call me Arnold."

"Arnold," the nurse repeated with a smile. "Arnold, how are you feeling today?"

"God has been good to me. The hip is really hurting today though. God has sent Doctor Tangle to fix that."

Sharon responded, "Arnold, on a scale of one to ten, what is the level of the pain in your hip?"

He answered fairly quickly, "I'd have to say eight. I haven't had any food or anything for pain since supper last night."

"That was my next question," the nurse said. "No food since before midnight. Do you need anything for pain?"

Mrs. Miller chimed in, "Arnold usually takes two aspirin at breakfast."

The nurse responded, "We can't do aspirin, since it's a blood thinner, but I could see about something else."

"I'll be all right," Mr. Miller said. "But before you leave, let us pray together." He took the nurse's hand, and Jolene and Keith quickly added their hands to form a circle of prayer.

"Precious God," Mr. Miller began, "I ask you to bless your servant, Sharon, today. Father, we daily feel your love and power working in our lives; care for her in her work this day, watch over her home and family, and show her glimpses of your love in the world around her. Thank You, Lord! In Jesus's name. Amen."

Tom wrote, "Your inside-out living is quite an inspiration to me. And others see it, too. Look at our increase in attendance and membership! Praise be to God!

Let me share a lesson I've been learning: You've got to share the load. When you let someone help you, and you encourage them in their work, we all benefit. You don't burn yourself out, and your helpers feel accepted and a valued part of the team.

God bless you this day! Pastor Tom Osborn."

Tom made copies of the card for each person that had been attending the Inside-Out Project meetings, and added a hand-written message to a few of them. After putting a stamp on each, he walked them out to the mailbox in front of the church.

Old Dominion looked practically full this morning. The happy chatter in the sanctuary of ninety-six people quieted as the pianist began the prelude.

The pastor's mind desperately groped to remember a comment someone had made to him just before he walked to his chair behind the pulpit. Who had it been?

Tom scanned the congregation. John Carter caught his eye, and he gave a slight nod of the head. That was who it was. Hallelujah! John wanted to make an announcement.

After the welcome, Tom Osborn said, "We've got a few important events coming up, but before I mention those, John Carter has something to share with us. John?"

John quickly made his way to the pulpit microphone.

"Many of you know," he started, "that I have a small prayer ministry going on at my workplace. I have a slotted container on my desk, a pig actually, that people drop prayer requests into, and I pray. God has blessed us with several miraculous answers to prayer. And that's a problem."

He paused, to add a little drama. All eyes were focused on him, evidently wondering how answered prayer could be a problem.

"Lately, the requests have really poured in. And people are expecting more of God. I need help! I need a couple people to help me pray. I don't want to give any of these faithful requests less attention than they really deserve. Please see me after church today if you are willing to help me carry this load. Thank you."

Rita could feel her knees trembling, but she wasn't sure why.

When Tom Osborn had invited members to visit the neighborhoods near the church with him, it sounded like a great idea. She had signed up for the next opportunity. Today.

So here she was, with the pastor, walking up the path to a two-story, white brick house. She tried to catch a full breath.

Tom reached to ring the door bell and then stepped back. He hadn't given her time to worry.

A balding man of slight build opened the door. Beaming widely, Rita started, "Good afternoon! I'm Rita Johnson."

Before she could say more, the man replied, "And I'm Sam Barney. Rita, you and my daughter went to high school together. How are you?"

She suddenly remembered the face. "Wow! I can't believe this!" Rita exclaimed. "Pastor, Mr. Barney's daughter, Debby, and I were a tennis doubles team at Belton High. I can't believe I didn't recognize the house."

Sam Barney swung the door open wider and invited them in. He said, "Nice to meet you, Pastor. Come in and tell me about your church."

The Barney family had always held membership at Belton First Baptist. Even so, Rita and Tom had a great visit, and Rita's confidence was bolstered for going on to the next houses.

CHAPTER 27

"Why, Mr. And Mrs. Barney," Rita exclaimed, "what a surprise! Excuse me, but I thought you'd be at First Baptist today."

Sam and Marie laughed. He replied, "Well, we just thought we'd come today, to repay you and your pastor for visiting us last Thursday."

Marie Barney joked, "You won't tell our pastor, will you?"

Sam interjected, "By the way, Reverend Osborn seems a little nervous today. Anything going on?"

Rita bent down closer to the guests and said quietly, "That tall, white-haired man sitting in the back on the other side is Lawton Bradley, our District Superintendent. He drops in every once in a while, unannounced, and Brother Tom wants everything to go just right today."

Rita continued, "Let me introduce you to these wonderful folks sitting in front of you."

The thirty-something couple in the next pew turned and smiled warmly at the visitors.

Rita said, "Sam and Marie Barney, this is Vince and Sarah McGill. They just moved to Belton from New Hampshire."

Mrs. McGill questioned, "Are you related to Debby Smith that works at the bank with me? I remember she said her maiden name was Barney."

Marie answered, "Yes, that's our daughter. So pleased to meet you. What brought you two to Belton?"

Vince answered, "I work for Cormac Paper, and I got a promotion that required me to move. But we love it here. And this is a great church. Brother Tom is really passionate about his love for God."

The pianist started the prelude, catching Tom Osborn visiting with some of the youth. He hurried to the front to take his place on the stage, snatching a quick glance in the direction of the District Superintendent.

What a day. What a Monday!

She wondered, *What have I gotten myself into?*

Helen slid the small recliner back out the front door of her soon-to-be shop, Just What You Need, and let it sit on its side on the sidewalk. She knew it would fit through the door. She just needed another hand or two.

With a stick she found nearby, Helen Adams managed to prop the door open. She wrapped her arms around the piece of furniture and tried again to maneuver it through the door.

A car slammed on its brakes, and Helen heard footsteps running in her direction.

"Need some help?"

Helen recognized Ricky, from her church.

"Thanks so much," she said. "I know this little chair will fit through this door, but I can't seem to watch every corner at once, and it keeps catching on something."

Ricky helped her pull the recliner back out the door.

"Here," he said, "you take the front end and I'll take the back."

Within a minute, the chair was in the door. They set it down next to a floor lamp.

"Helen, right?" Ricky asked. "I remember you joining the church a few weeks ago. I'm Ricky Temple."

"Helen Adams. I remembered your first name. I'm glad you stopped by when you did. This little brown recliner was wearing me out."

"Glad to help. So is this going to be your business? Looks like a little bit of everything."

"Very good!" Helen said. "That's just the impression I want people to have. Hence the name, Just What You Need. My grand opening is just a couple weeks away, and there's still a lot to do."

Ricky could smell coffee, and he spotted an urn nearby.

"Helen, what kind of coffee is that? It smells great!"

She looked in the direction of her coffee corner, beneath a sign that read Susan's Wild Bird Coffee II. "I'm trying out something called Jamaican Cove. It's really good."

"Tell you what," Ricky said, "this is my day off from Bestmart. If I can have a few cups of that coffee, I'll help you move things around for the rest of the day."

"Are you kidding?" she exclaimed. "Deal! Deal!"

❧

Lydia looked at the world globe on the public library desk. On a whim, she decided to see how close she could come to pinpointing Belton, Georgia.

She touched Georgia on the globe. Actually, even her small finger was big enough to cover most of the Peach State.

Lydia Michaelson thought about her recent ten-dollar giveaway, in which she asked each person to use her gift to help somebody else. They had done an amazing amount of good in the Belton area.

Looking at the globe, she thought, *Can't we do something to reach beyond this little spot?*

The denomination had missionaries around the globe. Lydia decided that sending special support to a missionary in Africa was the project Old Dominion needed.

"And I'm not going to do it all by myself," she proclaimed loudly. "Everyone is going to help me!"

"Shhhh!" A bespectacled librarian stared in her direction.

Oops. Lydia quietly slipped out the front door.

CHAPTER 28

July 16 promised to be a sunny, dry day. Keith put a lot of effort into arranging for the White House Paint Project, but he considered it a humble gift to God. He could never thank God enough for his new life.

Mary Eddy had at first declined Keith Slappey's offer to paint her old house. "This faded blue will be good enough for the ten or twenty years of life I've got left," she said.

But once Keith explained to her what a great benefit it would be to Old Dominion Church to work together on this project, she okayed his efforts. Her only provision was that he let her pay for the white paint.

For several weeks now, Keith had been asking friends, customers, and especially church members to help him on July 16. He had lined up ladders, rollers, and drop cloths. Freddy, owner of the Sports Bar, had a previous life as a house painter, and he advised Keith on everything he would need.

Now, if only ten or twelve people would show up to work!

As Sylvia was leaving work at Calvary Baptist, she spied Tom's car next to hers in the parking lot. He popped out of his car and called out, "Is it time for ice cream?"

"Sure," she answered. "I'll follow you to the Dairy Barn."

They bought matching strawberry sundaes and sat at the outdoor picnic table. He was smiling brightly, as he usually did lately.

"Remember Buddy Cooper, the truck driver I met at KJ's?" he asked. "He showed up at church Sunday. I meant to visit with him after church, but he had a half-dozen people around him by the time I got there. I expect he'll come back."

"That's great. Old Dominion is doing well, isn't it?"

"It really is. I've been using your tips on passing out encouragement. It's been a significant help."

He noticed that Sylvia just wasn't her joyful self today. "Something didn't go well today, I can tell."

"Oh, I guess it's no big deal. The chairman of the deacons stopped by to tell me there would be no pay raises again next year. Honestly, Tom, I just don't feel appreciated."

"I understand. The Lord will provide, you'll have enough money, but we all work together better when we encourage each other. You know I think you're the best Children's Minister in the whole world. Let me say a prayer."

"Thank you, Tom." Sylvia took his outstretched hand.

"Dear God, our king and our friend, I thank you for Sylvia and the love we share. Lord, please send someone with an encouraging word today. You know she loves your children, and seeks to serve you with her whole heart."

Sylvia squeezed Tom's hand. "Father in heaven, I thank you for Tom and the constant encouragement he brings me. Lord, restore my joy in the work you've put before me. In Jesus's name. Amen."

John Carter poured a cup of coffee and sat down at a small table in the Edison Fund break room. At the next table, there was an animated conversation in progress. John recognized Ralph as the one with his back to him.

Surely, this conversation was about Mr. Edison and his impending retirement. The president of the company, years ago, had set seventy as the mandatory retirement age. Now he would comply with his own rule.

Every employee seemed to know who ought to take over the reins of Edison Fund Insurance, but John had not heard the same name twice. The president's twin sons were both medical doctors, but neither had been involved in the family business. Two or three underwriters had over thirty years' experience. The Edisons also had a nephew that worked for a competitor.

"It was amazing," Ralph was saying.

The other man at the table replied, "It was the very next week? That's incredible."

John listened a little more closely now. He could not help being curious. "It really changed my ideas about prayer," Ralph said. "I just wrote on the paper, 'My son has been looking for a job for a long time, please pray for him,' dropped it in John's prayer pig, and I guess somebody prayed for it. Just a few days later, Kenny landed the best job he's ever had. It had to be the prayer."

John was stunned. A few weeks ago, this same guy was pressuring John to eliminate the prayer ministry. God has a sense of humor.

ॐ

"I've got a special sermon today," Reverend Tom Osborn said. "In fact, it's not a sermon, but a testimony, and it's not me. I've asked Ricky Temple to tell us his story. Ricky?"

Tom smiled and turned to Ricky, seated in the other pulpit chair on the stage.

Ricky never looked up. His eyes were closed, and he was quietly snoring.

"Ricky?"

Still no answer. People throughout the church began to chuckle.

Ricky jumped up and sprang to the pulpit. Tom adroitly got out of the way. Ricky blurted out, "Just kidding, y'all!"

Now laughter erupted all over, Ricky freely joining in.

"But I used to sleep in church all the time. You remember, don't you?" Ricky saw many heads nodding. "Never again! God has my complete attention now. I want to drink in everything God sends my way, the songs, the scriptures, your encouragement. Speak to me, God, 'cause I'm awake!"

Ricky slid the wireless microphone out of its clip and started pacing.

"For thirty-four years," he continued, "I wasn't listening to God. I didn't miss a Sunday service at Old Dominion unless I was out of town. But I was missing the best part of life.

"My life was falling apart," he continued. "Or I guess it wasn't falling together. Nothing was moving forward. Many of my friends were married, with a couple kids, buying a house. They were working toward a future. Me, I was just drifting through life. There were a lot of days I wondered why I was even taking up floor space."

Ricky was back at the pulpit now.

"The word that kept coming to mind was *lame*. I was living a lame life. Then, at our revival last February, Reverend Springstead kept talking about power— power to live inside out, power to reach out, power to change. It was a foreign concept to me, but I knew it was what I needed. And when he said this power lives in us, once we accept Jesus as our Savior, I knew what I had to do."

Ricky paused for a few seconds, knowing he was getting to the climax of his story. He owed it to God to finish well.

"All those years in church, awake or asleep, hadn't gotten the point across to me," he continued. "And here's the point: Jesus died on the cross to pay the penalty for our sins, and once we claim that payment for ourselves, he comes to live in us with power."

Applause and amens broke out in Old Dominion United Methodist Church.

He concluded, "I took Jesus up on that offer, found my purpose in life, and now my lame life is growing more powerful every day. Thank you."

CHAPTER 29

Belton College classes would begin in two days. Helen's shop, Just What You Need, bustled with activity on its first day of business.

"Another load of bookshelves, Helen," Hank Walton said, as he pushed in a hand truck laden with two-tier unfinished shelves. "I've still got twenty at the house. Maybe it'll be enough."

Helen replied, "I may need you to make a few more next week, if you have time. Seems that news about these shelves is going viral!"

Betty Carter had volunteered to help Helen in the store the first few days. The plan was to employ college students as soon as the semester started. Ricky, on vacation this week, had stopped by for coffee and now was lending a hand.

The yellow T-shirts advertising the store were selling briskly. Students all over the campus, by their attire, were proclaiming, "Just What You Need."

Helen was already plotting ways to keep the momentum going after the start of the semester. Next week was "Coffee Week," and she was giving out coupons for a free cup with every purchase of twenty dollars or more. Plus, anyone wearing a yellow Just

What You Need T-shirt would get ten per cent off their purchases on Tuesdays.

"You going back into the painting business, Freddy?" Ben Williams said. "I saw your truck in front of the paint store a lot last month."

The owner of Freddy's Sports Bar laughed. "No, those days are over," he said. "Spending every summer out in the heat on a long ladder gets old after awhile. I was helping your buddy, Keith, organize what he needed to paint a house. It was a big thing at his church."

"Yeah, I heard about that," Ben said. "They had so many people helping, they painted the whole place in a day. Have you seen the house?"

Freddy replied, "It's a little two-story, over on Boxwood Drive. A sweet, older lady lives there. She really couldn't afford to have the place painted, but Keith said she insisted on paying for the paint. I told the guy at the store to charge her two hundred bucks, and I'd pay the rest."

Freddy moved to wait on a new customer at the other end of the bar. Ben took another swallow from his beer and stared out the window the next few minutes. His mind wandered to the job offer his uncle had laid before him last week.

Ben had been at his present job for ten years. He was comfortable, and change was hard. But his uncle was offering him a big jump in salary, plus a lot more responsibility. He wasn't sure he was up to it.

"Ready for another beer?" Freddy said.

"No, not just yet. It's one of my thinking days."

"So, how'd you know about Keith's project? Did he ask you to help?"

Ben Williams seemed to squirm on the bar stool a little. He looked Freddy squarely in the eye.

"I heard it in church."

Freddy looked a little shocked. "You've been to church?"

Ben smiled sheepishly. "Yeah. Who would have thought it? But Ricky said he was giving a little testimony one Sunday at Old Dominion, and I snuck in to hear him. The guy's got more confidence lately, and I think church is where he got it."

"You going back?"

"I sneak in every week," he replied. "I walk in just after they start, sit in the back, and leave right after the sermon. If you give churches a chance, they'll be all over you."

❧

"Good morning, Rita and Mandy! Who have you brought to church with you this morning?" Betty Carter asked. "That is a gorgeous blouse you have on."

Rita quickly replied, "This is Shannon, a classmate of Mandy's, Betty. We all stayed up playing Monopoly until two this morning."

"Ms. Betty," Mandy said, "I think you like Shannon's pink top because it's the same color as your dress!"

"You're right, Mandy. So glad to have you with us this morning, Shannon."

"Thank you, ma'am," came the reply as Betty moved on to greet others.

Susan Clark was just getting settled in a pew when Betty spotted her.

"Susan, you're just the person I wanted to see," she said.

Betty bent down and tilted her head toward Susan.

"Now, tell me, what do you see?"

Susan looked at the side of Betty's head with a puzzled look and said, "What am I supposed to see?"

"That John and I have tomatoes coming out of our ears," she said with a laugh. "Can I bring you some tomorrow?"

"I'd be glad to have some. I'll be at the coffee shop every day this week."

"Good," Betty said. "Thanks for helping us out."

John Carter watched his wife move about the congregation. By the time worship started and she sat down next to him in the pew, Betty had greeted twenty-two people.

CHAPTER 30

Another bag of trash in the road! Lydia Michaelson hated to see pickup trucks thoughtlessly driving along with bags of trash in the back, knowing that a good gust from a passing transfer truck would lift the trash onto the street.

Lydia looked for a place to turn around. *If nobody else cares, I certainly do!* she thought.

When traffic was clear, Lydia did a tight U-turn on the four-lane and parked as far to the right as she could. She snared the bag of trash from the highway and took it to her Mercedes.

She popped the trunk open, slipped the black bag in, and closed it again.

As Lydia turned, she saw a blue SUV bearing down on her. The driver was looking down at something in the front seat.

"Dear God!" she screamed and leaped onto the car trunk.

The SUV's driver glanced up, veered left, but not in time.

❧

Reverend Bob Pearson, of Belton First Baptist Church, sat in Tom's office. His six-foot-four-inch frame carried its three hundred pounds well.

Pearson sat glaring at Tom Osborn across his desk.

Tom smiled and said, "So good to meet you, Brother Bob. What can I do for you this fine morning?"

The Baptist pastor leaned forward in his seat. Louder than necessary, he started, "Mr. Osborn, are you aware that the city of Belton is filled with unchurched people? More than sixty percent of our population has no church affiliation whatsoever. Our city needs Christians who will reach out to the *unchurched* and tell them about Jesus."

Tom replied enthusiastically, "Oh, yes! I agree. In fact, we're visiting up and down the streets near our church every week. We certainly share your concern for the lost."

Pastor Osborn relaxed slightly. Perhaps he had misjudged his visitor's attitude. It seemed they were kindred spirits.

Now Reverend Pearson grew sterner.

He continued. "Your 'visiting up and down the streets' is what I came to discuss. Mr. Osborn, there are enough unchurched to interest you Methodists without bothering my people. The sheep know the voice of their own shepherd, Jesus said. All others are liars and thieves. You need to quit stealing my sheep and develop your own flock!"

Tom Osborn could feel his face start to rise in temperature. He didn't care for his brother pastor's accusations, and it aggravated him to be called *Mr. Osborn.*

"Excuse me, brother," Tom replied. "As Jacob told Laban, search what I have and show me anything here that's yours."

Reverend Pearson brandished a small yellow card from his suit pocket.

"I'm told by very reliable sources that Susan Clarkson is attending here," he said. "A young lady named Mary Eddy has started attending here and has stopped mailing in her tithe."

Tom interjected, "Young, you say?"

"Don't interrupt!" Pearson spat back. "Even one of my deacons, Sam Barney, attended your church, after you had the audacity to visit him in his home. I tell you, young man, God's kingdom will not be increased by swapping believers from one house of worship to another."

Reverend Tom Osborn said nothing for a full minute. The temper he'd harbored in his younger days fought to slide back in just then, but Tom called on the Holy Spirit to bar the door. For his part, Reverend Bob Pearson sat satisfied that he'd made his point.

Finally Tom spoke.

"Brother Bob, I want you to know that I love and appreciate you. Your church is a beacon for Christ in our community. I'm sorry for any misunderstanding between us.

"Let me set you straight on a few facts. Susan Clarkson does not attend here. We have a Susan Clark, who had previously been an unattending Christian for many years, and she has never mentioned where she used to attend.

"Mary Eddy is in her eighties and has never been inside your church; she picked your church out of the phone book as a place to send her monthly tithe before she started attending Old Dominion. She was desperate to give thanks to God.

"And the Barneys attended only one Sunday, basically to encourage an old friend of their daughter."

Tom stood up and held the door open for his guest.

"You need not worry about me and my church, brother. Your sheep love their shepherd, because he knows them by name."

Troubled by his recent visitor, Tom decided to grab coffee at KJ's Cafe. Heading down Gilbertville, he could see a police car ahead, directing traffic as a wrecker loaded a demolished car.

Hope it wasn't anyone I know, he thought.

As the pastor eased past the smashed luxury car, nothing looked familiar.

Except the license plate, LM 1.

"That's Lydia's car!" he shouted.

Helen walked up to the bar and waited for the bartender's attention.

She could feel the eyes of the other patrons on her, but she didn't glance around. Was she dressed appropriately, in blue jeans and a frilly blouse?

"What'll you have, lady?" Freddy called from ten feet away.

"Just a Coke, please," Helen answered.

She could hear a few snickers around her.

When Freddy brought her beverage, she said, "I'm looking for Ricky Temple's Bible study."

The bartender jerked his thumb toward a room behind him. "High Life. They're just getting ready to start."

Lydia was sitting in a chair when her pastor entered her hospital room.

"Before you ask," she said, "torn ligaments, about six weeks' recovery. A very close call."

CHAPTER 31

Hank, Mandy, and Rita headed up the walkway of the two-story brick home. As Rita pushed the doorbell, Hank had a momentary glimpse of someone peeking through the blinds.

They heard a voice quietly call out, "Mom, somebody's here!"

In a moment, the door swung open to a tall, red-headed lady and a preteen strawberry blond.

"Hi, Mandy," the girl said. "Is this your family? This is my mom."

"I'm Betty Lancer," the mother spoke. "I'm glad to meet you."

"Welcome to the neighborhood," Hank said, proffering a plastic tray of brownies. Before he could say more, Mandy stepped forward.

"Sheila, this is my granddaddy I told you about. He writes for the newspaper."

Betty looked at Rita and reached out her hand. "And you must be Mandy's mother," she said.

"I'm Rita Johnson," she replied. "It's nice to meet you, Betty. I rent a couple of rooms in Hank and Mandy's house, so I'm part of the household. Hank thought it would be good if we could meet our new neighbors."

"Won't you all please come in?" Betty asked, as she stepped back and opened the door wide. "You'll have to come back when Mandy's parents can be with you."

Mandy said to her classmate, "Sheila, I made the brownies. I know they're good, because I tried one."

The birds were the same, with their bright jungle colors. Almost.

Tom looked around as he chewed on a bite of bagel in Susan's Wild Bird Coffee Shop II, which took up a third of Helen Adams's business establishment. A toucan near the cash register played a harmonica. Above the rest room door, a parrot seemed to be typing on a keyboard. With brush in claw, a parakeet gazed in a mirror. Two macaws were either dancing or shaking hands, he wasn't sure which. Every one of the thirty birds seemed busy at something.

"More Jalapeño Dark?" Brittany asked, suddenly standing next to the pastor's small table.

He replied, "Yes, thank you. Better make it my last cup, though. I don't want to be wide-eyed at eleven tonight."

As she returned with his refill, Brittany said, "That's about the time I'll be starting my Pol Sci paper. You might as well be awake with the rest of us!"

Helen entered at the other end of Just What You Need, carrying two small boxes and some mail. Spying Tom Osborn fifty feet away, she waved and headed in his direction.

"I see you've met Brittany, Pastor," she said. "It's been a hectic two weeks since my grand opening, but it's been a lot less stressful since Brittany started working last week. She's a star."

Brittany interjected, "I worked at a coffee shop when I was in high school. The rest of the store was easy to learn."

"How many college students work here?" Tom asked.

"Well," Helen replied, "until I expand my hours of operation, just three. I practically live here, eight to eight every day, Monday through Friday. I keep a second worker at all times. Brittany works about twenty-eight hours, and Nick and Daniel cover the rest. Great kids! You'll have to meet the guys."

"I'm glad the school colors are yellow and black," Tom said. "Just What You Need T-shirts are everywhere!"

Helen smiled. "Coincidence?"

The organist was settling in at her instrument. The prelude would start in just a few minutes.

Leo Bubber could remember the day when nurses were easily distinguishable by their ghost-white uniforms. Even so, anyone could tell that the six ladies wearing various colors of hospital scrubs in the second pew were probably nurses.

"Welcome!" Leo said. "I'm glad you're here. Let me tell you, our nurses here at Anderson General are the best in the world. I'm not exaggerating. I read a report online last week that compared hospitals in our state, and the nursing staff at our own hospital was rated number one. Thank you for doing such a great job."

Leo's comment caused the whole row to smile.

"Yes, sir, news of that report is the hottest news in the facility this week," a gray-haired nurse in purple said. "We're really proud."

Leo suddenly remembered. "I'm sorry, I forgot to introduce myself. I'm Leo Bubber, and that's my wife, Catherine, over yonder in the lavender dress."

Another nurse said, "I'll bet you're related to Lydia Michaelson."

"Why do you say that?"

"She is why we're here today," a slim nurse in green said. "She tells all the nurses she sees, since she's been in the hospital, that we're the best in the world. And she says the same thing about the people of this church, that y'all are the best. So we came to see if it's true."

"And?" Leo said.

All six nurses chimed in together, "You are!"

CHAPTER 32

The Sunday night post-worship meeting of the Inside-Out Project began with a question. "Why do new people come to Old Dominion?" Tom asked.

Hank raised his hand. "Most of the time," he said, "at least in the past year, they come because they're invited."

Maxine called out, "They come because we care enough to knock on their door."

"People are looking for something," Fred said. "This is not usually the first thing they've tried. For some, it might be the last resort. If this doesn't work, they will just quit trying, and let life take them wherever it wants to."

After a slight pause, Tom said, "I wonder if we're doing all God wants us to do. When we visit, are we offering a clear path to Jesus, or does it sound like we are inviting them to a friendly club? People looking for a real solution need to suspect they can find it at our church."

Rita tentatively raised her hand. "Pastor, I think I see where you're going with this. You want us to add a little 'Jesus' to our invitation."

"Doesn't that seem reasonable?" Tom said. "God makes it no secret that Jesus is the Way, Jesus is the answer. Only through him will we have the strength to do the right thing, which is really what folks are trying to do. People want abundant life, but we know you just can't do it without that holy strength within."

"I hope you're not expecting us to memorize a chapter in Romans," Fred inserted. "That wouldn't feel natural to me."

Hank said, "If I just talked about how God helps me each day, I think I could make it fit into a normal conversation."

"Think so?" Tom asked, with a smile.

He was on his own this week. For the past two weeks, Jolene Miller had been showing Keith all the details of how she cleaned the church, preparing him for taking over the job. As soon as Arnold Miller was recovered from his hip surgery, the Millers planned to do some traveling.

Actually, this would be the only week Keith Slappey maintained Old Dominion by himself. He had asked Sam and Betty Lou Anderson, the couple that joined the church the same day Keith did, to help. They were glad to be given a place in which to serve. The two Anderson sons would help by mowing the lawn.

This week, Keith would do just the basics. Next week, he would start on the jobs that rarely got done, like washing the windows and dusting the chandeliers.

I wonder if it's possible, he thought, *for every person in the church to have a way to be involved. Surely there are others, like the Andersons, who would gladly serve the Lord if they were just asked.*

❧

"Hello, Betty," said Fran. "Please come in."

Betty Carter stepped inside the home of Fran Smith and her son, Frankie.

"I've brought you some more tomatoes," Betty said.

At the mention of tomatoes, Frankie seemed to appear out of nowhere. "Wow, thank you so much, Mrs. Carter," he said. "Those last tomatoes you brought us made some incredible sandwiches."

"You are certainly welcome, Frankie," she said. "This Rutgers variety does seem to be sweeter than others we've tried."

"Betty, come sit in the kitchen and have some lemonade with us. It's so nice to have a visitor," Fran said.

The three moved to the kitchen, where Fran promptly poured Betty a tumbler of lemonade.

"Fran," Betty said, "it amazes me when I think back on how shy I used to be. I was okay teaching little children at school, but once I got home in the afternoon, I never stepped foot outside."

Frankie spoke up. "I'm just the opposite."

Fran added, "His teachers tell me he rarely talks in class. At home, he talks up a storm. Betty, how did you get over your shyness?"

Betty Carter prayed the world's shortest prayer—*Lord, help!*—then answered her neighbors.

"I just decided that, since I'm a Christian, and with God nothing is impossible, I'd ask God to help me get over my shyness. It was a real miracle. Within just a couple weeks, I felt comfortable talking with anybody and everybody."

"Betty," Fran said, "that time we went to your church, the pastor talked about becoming a Christian and having a relationship with God, but it sounded too easy."

Betty took a long drink of lemonade, and then replied, "God has a way that this world and our lives ought to follow. We have our own ideas that ruin his plan. If we believe in Jesus's death as payment for our disobedience, our sin, God considers the bill as paid, and his very presence comes to live in us from that day on. It's easy, but it can be a hard step for people to take."

Frankie cleared his throat, and then said, "It's not hard for us. Mom and I have been talking about this since we met all those people at your church. We want a relationship with God."

"Betty, can you tell us what to pray?" Fran said.

CHAPTER 33

"How's the 'High Life' going, Ricky?" Tom asked. Ricky Temple sat up in his chair in the pastor's office.

"July was great," he said. "The Bible study group was new, and we had eight or ten people a night. August was down to six, and for September, so far we've had three or four a night."

Tom Osborn leaned back in his chair. He asked, "Who are your regulars?"

"I guess my most regular attender has been my buddy, Ben Williams, though he's always late, and he's always carrying a beer. The past few weeks, Helen Adams has been with us. I appreciate her support."

"Ben was the one you really wanted to reach, wasn't he?"

"Yeah," Ricky replied, "I can't tell that he's getting anything out of the High Life. But he keeps coming back."

"It's been great having him in church."

"I appreciated his coming the day I gave my testimony. Too bad he didn't come back."

"Oh no, he's been here every week."

"Are you kidding? I haven't seen him."

"He always slips in a few minutes late and leaves just after the benediction. That's why I started doing the benediction from the back of the church, so I could greet him before he leaves."

Ricky didn't know what to say next.

The pastor continued. "Sounds like you should consider setting an ending date for the study at the bar. Maybe two or three more weeks."

Ricky pondered the suggestion for a few moments.

"You're probably right," he said. "I guess I would miss standing in front of people, talking about God. Maybe I should get in line to teach a Sunday school class."

Tom Osborn dug through a pile of papers on his desk, until he found a light blue flyer.

"Ricky, take a look at this," he said. "There's a class coming up, at Belton First Methodist, for lay speaker training. I think you ought to go." He handed the flyer to Ricky.

After studying the sheet for a moment, Ricky replied, "Is this for guys that are thinking about going into the ministry?"

The pastor grinned. "No, not only potential ministers. It helps anyone that wants to do a better job of sharing Christ.

"Ricky, the way our church is growing, I may soon need a part-time assistant to help me encourage our congregation. Sometimes I feel like I've got a hundred-pound dog on a leash and he's suddenly started chasing a squirrel. Right now I'm managing all right, but who knows what's coming up?"

John Carter stopped at his desk on the way to the break room for his first cup of coffee. He took a quick glance at the sign-up sheet for the prayer study he was starting next Monday at lunch.

Becky and Fred had signed up the first day. That was no surprise, since God had answered John's prayers for them in the early days of the 'prayer pig' ministry. Freida's name was next. Ralph had also signed up, yesterday. Those four would be enough for a good class. Mr. Edison had reserved a small consultation room for John's use, showing his support.

One more name had been added today, a Ben Williams. "Must be Mr. Edison's new assistant," John mused.

"Something's still missing," Helen said as she brought Tom's morning bagel.

"Are you sure?" the pastor asked.

He looked around Helen's store. There were still a few bookshelves on display and several plastic crates, essentials for college students. Some good, secondhand upholstered chairs shared a corner with various styles of folding chairs. Posters lined the walls. There was a rack of the famous bright yellow Just What You Need T-shirts.

Tom asked, "Where did you get the pieces of carpet?"

Rectangular pieces of carpet of various sizes stood in a slightly precarious stack near the door. The largest was about four foot square, the smallest maybe eighteen inches by two feet.

Helen said, "I've got a college friend who now manages a carpet store here in Belton. They often have leftover remnants from carpeting a house. If they are long strips, Mike will cut them down to smaller sizes."

"Do they sell?"

"Since Belton College dorm rooms have bare floors, I thought these scraps might be popular. I was right."

"And you're sure there's something missing? By the way, you've got some incredibly innovative posters for sale of scenes from Belton and the college. Where do you buy them?"

Helen laughed. "Famous artist. I wander around, taking pictures, and then have them blown up to poster size at Village Copy.

"Tom, I really want to think of more ways of living inside out. I've been trying to meet the needs of the college and the community, but I think what I'm missing is a Bible study. I need it oriented toward kids eighteen to twenty-five."

Pastor Tom Osborn took a bite of bagel. He thought through his weekly schedule.

"No offense, Tom, but I need somebody who can put the Bible in simple terms. From my experience, college kids often are Bible illiterate."

"Do you know Ricky Temple?" Tom replied. "I'll bet he would be just what you're looking for."

Tom thought perhaps Helen's face reddened slightly.

"Helen, would you like me to ask Ricky for you?"

"No, that's all right. We see each other nearly every night."

CHAPTER 34

B en sensed this was a special day. God seemed to confirm it, for the prelude the pianist played was Grandma Edison's favorite hymn, "Morning Has Broken." It had received much more than its fair share of attention when she had been the musician here, many years ago.

Ben grew up in a family that attended church a few times a year. How had he gotten away from that? Maybe Grandma's death had something to do with it, when Ben was fifteen. That's when his parents started attending other churches. Gasoline and perfume contributed; he got his own car and started dating at sixteen, and late Saturday dates made it easy to sleep in on Sundays.

Twenty-five years later, God was still here, waiting patiently for his wayward child.

The pastor stood up to speak. "Good morning! I'm glad you're here!"

The crowd responded with a vibrant, "Good morning!"

From the choir, Helen Adams called out, "Pastor, you stole my greeting!" A dozen people in the crowd chuckled, and Tom grinned widely.

After a few announcements of upcoming church events, the pastor announced, "You'll see in your bulletin that we have two baptisms this morning. Fran and Frankie, please come to the front."

As the Smiths came forward, Tom added, "It may be that others of you would like to join the Smith family this morning, in either baptism or joining the church. If so, you come, too!"

All eyes in the choir immediately opened wide. Ben Williams jumped from his pew, as if booted by an angel, and rushed forward.

Ben whispered to the pastor, "I want to join. I was baptized here as an infant." Tom nodded his head.

Tom addressed the congregation. "I invite any family or close friends of these three wonderful children of God. Perhaps you'd like to come up in support of them as they make their commitment to God and the church."

Betty Carter immediately joined Fran and Frankie at the altar rail. Ricky Temple and Keith Slappey also hurried forward.

"Dear friends," Tom continued, "when people are baptized or join our church, it is also an important opportunity for each of us to remember the vows taken and to recommit ourselves to God's service. Please turn now to the baptism and membership service in the front of your hymnal."

After the benediction at Old Dominion, it seemed like every single person of the 104 people in attendance took the opportunity to shake hands with the Smiths and Ben Williams. Hank Walton and Rita were at the end of the line, a full fifteen minutes after the first greeting.

"Ben, we're so glad you joined us," Hank said. "You may not remember me, but my wife and I kept the nursery when you were a kindergartner. My wife is gone now, but I remember that she loved your hair. It was really blond and curly."

"I think I remember that," Ben said. "Was her name Jeanette? She loved to get down in the floor and play with us."

"I do miss Jeanette. Ben, how about joining Rita, Mandy, and me for lunch at our house? That is, if you don't already have plans."

"Thank you, I'd be glad to come," Ben said. "I guess I need to get know my new church family."

Keith found a quiet corner in the pub and put in his order for a double cheeseburger and fries. He got out a yellow pad and wrote down the names of people helping him clean the church.

Keith had discovered that new members of Old Dominion kept their excitement for the church if they were allowed to help in some way. What could he connect Ben and the Smiths with? Keith was only in charge of buildings and grounds.

He began his list. The two Anderson boys were cutting the grass. Len Parrot did all the string trimming. Rita was a master at taking care of the shrubbery. Maybe that took care of everything outside; he'd have to think about it.

Sam and Betty Lou Anderson were cleaning the sanctuary. One day, Catherine Bubber had asked to clean

the bathrooms—"to make them sparkle one time"—
and had taken over ever since. Tommy Chisholm was
six foot four, so Keith had asked him to be in charge
of changing light bulbs, inside the building and out.
"Sure," Tommy said, "and I'll be glad to help with any
other high-reaching job you can think of."

Buddy Cooper had just volunteered to keep all the
windows clean, inside and out. He used to do that for
a living.

Maybe Keith would ask Ben to help vacuum the
Sunday school rooms.

❧

"Granddaddy, thank you for such a great lunch!"
Mandy said. "Meat loaf, macaroni and cheese, broccoli
casserole, and then pound cake with strawberries for
dessert—I think our company was impressed."

"Remember, it was Rita that made the pound cake.
Thank you, Rita," Hank said.

Rita was just coming from the kitchen, after having
washed the dishes.

"Ben Williams certainly seems like a fine, level-
headed man," she said. "I like him. He said our church
has helped him find a purpose in life. I know a lot of
men his age who are still looking."

Mandy said, "When I get married, I'm going to
make sure my boyfriend knows Jesus before he gets the
first date."

CHAPTER 35

Boxwood Drive came as close as it ever had to a traffic jam on Saturday night. Too many people slowed to look at the spectacle of fifty white folding chairs on Mary Eddy's front lawn.

The four-color flyer distributed last week proclaimed "Church Turned Inside Out" and worship at 6 p.m. on the corner of Boxwood and Gilbertville. Already, at 5:45, Vince and Sarah McGill were singing new Christian lyrics to a popular rock song and were attracting an audience.

Mary Eddy and Ricky Temple stood nearby. "Young man, what are you preaching about tonight?" Mrs. Eddy directed toward Ricky.

Ricky smiled and said, "What I know best: how to take a messed up life with no direction and point it toward Jesus."

"Can I have a copy of it when you get done?"

Ricky fanned through the pages of his Bible, revealing no papers or notes.

"I've only got a rough outline in my head," he said. "I'm depending on God and the listeners for what order I present things in."

The McGills continued to their next song. Fifteen to twenty people were milling around, drinking the free sodas and eating brownies and chips that one of the neighbors had brought.

"It looks like I'll get to meet more of my neighbors tonight." Mrs. Eddy said. "Most of these folks only come out to cut their grass."

Lydia scanned the empty sanctuary. She tried to imagine the room with no pulpit, no altar rails, and no communion table.

"I think it would work," Fred Browner, the chairman of the trustees, said. "It would double the size of our existing fellowship hall, plus there would be a stage for any kind of dinner theater, talent show, or whatever."

Lydia walked to the west side and stared out the windows of the double doors. The grassy two-acre lot never had been used very much, though it was a much larger lawn than that on the east side of Old Dominion.

"And you think," she said, "that two million would be adequate for a two-hundred-fifty seat sanctuary?"

Reverend Lawton Bradley presided over the smallest district in the state, but the one with the most thousand-member United Methodist churches. Bradley's eight-year tenure as District Superintendent had been a time of remarkable growth, especially for the big churches.

Tom Osborn sat across from him in a corner booth at Freddy's Sports Pub.

"You really have done well at Old Dominion, Tom," Lawton said. "Let me see, you have gone from sixty average Sunday morning attendance to one hundred five, and you've gained thirty-eight members, all since February."

Tom replied, "William Springstead should get a lot of credit for our growth. He did a tremendous revival for us in February, and we've been flying high ever since. I didn't know people could be so revived by a revival."

The waiter arrived with their unsweetened tea. "Do you need a minute, gentlemen, or are you ready to order?"

The white-haired superintendent spoke up. "This young man needs a steak, and I've heard this pub has a tremendous rib eye. I'll have mine medium well. How about you, Tom? I'm paying today."

"Well," he said, "I was thinking spaghetti, but you've just changed my mind. I'd like my rib eye well done, baked potato, and a house salad with Italian dressing."

Reverend Bradley added, "Sounds good, but make my dressing ranch, thank you."

The waiter wrote busily, nodded, and then left.

"Tom," Lawton Bradley said, "revival aside, you have shown remarkable ability as a pastor in the sixteen months you've been here. Tell me more about how you've led the church to reach out. Old Dominion was like any other small church just a short time ago, slowly shrinking and worried about whether they'd have enough to pay the bills."

For the next twenty minutes, Tom Osborn described to his district superintendent how Old Dominion United Methodist Church had turned inside out. He told about the key individuals who had made dramatic changes in their lives, and how the change had been contagious. The older man continually emphasized the encouragement the pastor must have provided, and how essential that was to the process. Reverend Osborn admitted that he'd been a good cheerleader, but that it arose naturally out of his love for the congregation.

As Lawton cut into his apple pie, he glanced quickly at the nearby tables. No one seemed to be listening.

He proceeded. "Tom, have you heard of Sunnydale Church?"

The young pastor responded, "Yes, sir, that's the new church in Collegetown that's doing so well, isn't it?"

"That's right. Phenomenal. They've gone from zero to three hundred members in just four years. Dale Rentz knows what he's doing."

After a short pause, he continued.

"But he's about done all he can without an associate pastor."

Tom could see what was coming next and couldn't help squirming a little in his chair.

"Tom, you are just the kind of associate Dale needs. What you're doing at Old Dominion would translate well to Sunnydale. It would nearly double your present salary. Of course, the bishop would have to approve the hire, but he and I are already in agreement on this. I want you to earnestly pray about this. The position would start in January."

All Tom would later remember was being speechless for the rest of the meal.

CHAPTER 36

"Cast all your cares on him, for he cares for you," Ricky read. "I'm thinking this fits in with other Bible verses about stress, like 'Come unto Me, all who are weary and heavy-laden, and I will give you rest.'"

Billy, a freshman, said, "Okay, everybody says stress kills, and all that, but let's just clarify what the problem is with stress. Can't it be, like, an incentive?"

All fifteen chairs in Just What You Need's coffee shop were in use at tonight's Bible study, one more than last week. A free cup of coffee had surely been the primary attraction for some.

"I need pressure to force me to get things done sometimes," Janine said. "But still, I don't like stress."

An Asian student, Honey, spoke next. "Is it possible to separate the harmful part of stress from the discipline it brings? Do you know what I mean?"

"Now you're getting at it," Ricky said. "God offers to take the care part, the wearying, heavy load part of your stress. You could handle your responsibilities much better if the worry part of stress wasn't there. The worry part throws things out of focus."

Helen, the proprietor, spoke up. "There is always going to be too much to do at college. If God offers to relieve me of feeling stressed out, I can get more done.

That's a good enough reason for anybody to give God control of his life."

"By the way," Helen added, "a church friend sent over a batch of chocolate chip cookies. Anybody want one?"

It was Ed and Edna time.

Each year at the end of October, John and Betty Carter could expect a visit from his parents, Ed and Edna. The elder Carters took a swing through New England each fall, searching for brilliant displays of the changing foliage. Then they would travel south, to celebrate Ed's birthday with his son and his wife, Betty.

"You know, John," Ed said, "sometimes I wish we didn't travel. Oh, it's been nice seeing more of the USA and meeting new people. When we get home, though, we always find we've missed something important.

"Last fall, our live-in neighbors finally got married, and we didn't know it until just a month ago. The church held a confirmation class for the kids, and fifteen of them joined the church at once, and we never knew. Two years ago, our preacher's wife lost thirty pounds while we were on our fall trip and dyed her hair, and we thought he'd divorced and remarried."

John had to laugh. "So Dad, you don't recommend retirement?"

"Well, son," he said, "it's not all it's cracked up to be. I think I'd rather travel less and work more for the Lord in our church. Maybe get to know some of the young fathers better and help them along as kind of a mentor."

"You know, Dad," John said, "Mom was telling me the same kind of thing yesterday."

"What!?" Ed replied. "I thought we were doing all this traveling because *she* wanted to!"

After a few sips of coffee, Ed continued. "We've been retired for fifteen years now, and we've seen every state in the union. I'm ready to settle down. Maybe I need to go back to work."

᷈

"This is incredible chicken, Rita," Ben said. "What did you call it again?"

"Thank you, Ben," she said. "This recipe is chicken francais. It's only the second time I've made it. Mandy and Hank were so thrilled with it the first time that I decided it was good enough for company."

Hank added, "Rita is getting to be quite the cook. She's not afraid to try something new."

"I'm really glad you invited me," Ben spoke to Rita. "I don't go to much trouble for myself. I can make a great sandwich, but a real recipe would be an all-day project."

"Granddaddy," Mandy ventured, "should I say Ben or Mr. Ben?"

Their guest interrupted. "Please call me Ben, Mandy. Y'all are my church family."

"Okay, Ben," Mandy responded. "I like that better. Do you have a family in Belton?"

"Not a lot," he said. "My parents are no longer living, and I don't have any sisters or brothers. I work for my uncle at Edison Fund Insurance."

Mandy said, "We're like that, too."

Ben Williams looked a little puzzled.

"Oh, I almost forgot the dessert," Rita said. "Mandy, come help me get the ice cream and pie ready."

The two ladies slipped off to the kitchen.

"We are a pretty unique household, Ben," Hank said. "A few years ago, our daughter died in a car wreck. She was divorced at the time, and Mandy's father had no room for his daughter in his new marriage. So Jeannette and I adopted her. Then, two years ago, my wife died. Rita is actually a close friend of Mandy, a wonderful, fun person.

"Believe it or not, God pushed me to invite Rita to come live in this big house with us, and it's been great. Mandy needed a female influence I couldn't provide.

"And in case you ever wonder, there's nothing romantic between the two of us. I think of her more as a daughter."

The kitchen door swung open, as Mandy entered with a tray laden with pieces of pie and crystal dishes of ice cream.

"Would anyone like coffee?" Rita asked.

Hank typed away at his next newspaper column. He heard the door open. Mandy, in her pajamas, took a seat next to his desk.

"Got an idea for my column?"

"No, I've been thinking about Rita. I really love having her here with us."

"So do I. She's a wonderful Christian lady."

"Granddaddy, being a man, you may not have noticed it, but she's really in love this time. She gets all nervous when Ben is around."

Hank stifled his amusement. "I did notice things were different this time. Do you think we should approve?"

"Oh, yes! He's great. He's handsome, and he has a good job. And Ricky says he's turned his life around, and sincerely loves Jesus."

"I like that last part best."

"So I was thinking, Granddaddy. We want Rita to be happy. I'm learning to think inside out. If things get really serious, and Ben asks her to marry him, it'll be okay. You and I can do all right, just the two of us. She's already taught me a lot, and she'll still be my friend, so I'd be able to call her and ask her things anytime."

Hank stood up and pulled Mandy into his arms. "You are just one incredible person. Yes, we'd be all right."

CHAPTER 37

The denomination's bimonthly newspaper proclaimed, "Collegetown's Sunnydale Thrives." The lead article told the story of the amazing growth of Dale Rentz's startup church. Tom especially noted the line, "looking forward to hiring a new associate pastor in January."

The district superintendent really wanted a decision from Tom this week on his offer. This was the way his career was supposed to work, wasn't it? Begin with a 'starter' church like Red Oaks, move to a small, declining church and get it showing some growth, like he had at Old Dominion, then on to something bigger like the associate at Sunnydale.

The now-sixteen-and-a-half months Tom had pastored at Old Dominion Church had been happy months for him and extremely satisfying. The kingdom of God was expanding here. This church shone God's glorious light to the community.

How could he leave Belton and Old Dominion? It would be like a mother leaving her six-week-old baby to return to the workforce. Tom never understood how young mothers managed to do that.

But it happened all the time.

The most relevant fact to Tom was that Collegetown was several hours away from Helmsville.

The slightly overweight gentleman occasionally stared at Ricky Temple from the other end of the bar. Ricky smiled back, but he kept most of his attention on the wide-screen TV high on the wall. The Falcons rarely appeared on Monday night football. It was great to share it with his old friends, Ben and Keith.

The Falcons ground away at the Saints, keeping the ball in the hands of their running backs instead of passing. Great strategy! The Saints' defense was wearing down.

Ricky felt a tap on his shoulder, and turned. The man from the other end of the bar said, "I finally realized why you look familiar. You're the guy that preached at that outdoor church service on my street."

Ricky grinned and heartily shook his visitor's hand. "Good to see you! So you live on Boxwood Drive?"

"Yeah," the man replied. "Great sermon. My girlfriend and I meant to come to Old Dominion last Sunday, but we lay in bed too long. We'll try again this Sunday."

"Great," Ricky replied. "I'll be looking for you."

The other man seemed to be searching for the right words to say next. After a few seconds, he said, "Say, I'm a little surprised to see you here, in a bar."

"Me and Freddy go way back. Great food."

His conversation partner stared at Ricky's empty glass.

Ricky responded, "Coca-Cola."

Madge Randall had never expected the Book House to be a really profitable business. Madge and Leo had envisioned their store as a way to get out of the house in their retirement.

One day three years ago, Keith Slappey showed up, looking for a job. Leo decided they should give the kid a shot. It was their best decision ever.

Keith had a mind like a card catalog! Within weeks, he could tell you the exact location, within inches, of every book in the store. He read voraciously when he wasn't working, and he soon knew the plot of nearly every book on every shelf.

His recommendations for books they should buy were always sound. Madge had a few questions on his latest list though.

"Keith," Madge said, "I think we'd be stepping over the line with these two latest books you've requested. The C.S. Lewis book, *Mere Christianity*, is basically the author's defense of his Christian faith. Lee Strobel's *The Case for Christ* is about how he became a Christian, isn't it? We do our best to only carry fiction."

"Yes, ma'am," Keith said, "I see your point. I thought maybe *Mere Christianity* would supplement the *Chronicles of Narnia* and *Space Trilogy* books by Lewis that are selling so well."

Madge said, "Is there another fiction book by the same author?"

"*The Screwtape Letters* comes to mind," Keith said.

"Let's buy that," Madge replied. "Now, what about the Strobel book?"

"No good reason," Keith said. "It's not fiction. I guess I just got excited about what God is doing in my life."

Madge decided, at that very moment, that she and Leo had to visit Keith's church that Sunday. His religion had made Keith a better person and a better employee over the last several months, and she wanted to find out more about it.

The happy chatter before the worship service was instigated by eight people wearing red badges, Betty Carter's corps of church greeters. They were definitely happiness ambassadors, and they were having more fun than anyone else.

Beth Williams looked from the choir loft of Old Dominion at the friendly crowd, and she had to chuckle at her insistent feeling of jealousy. She wished she had a red badge.

But she also loved singing in the choir, helping lead the congregation in praising God.

Besides, you could see things going on in the congregation from up here that most never knew happened!

The fight was over. Lydia had not gotten everything she wanted.

The board of trustees accepted her offer to pay for the building of a new sanctuary for Old Dominion United Methodist Church on the lot west of the present building. They insisted though that the other members should pay for the cost of converting the present sanctuary to a more spacious fellowship hall.

Oh, well. It was only a battle. She had won the war.

CHAPTER 38

John had not even thought about retirement. He had grown up in the days when people retired at sixty-five. His parents had both retired at that age. Since John's parents had visited two weeks ago though, his outlook had changed.

"I think I'd rather travel less and work more for the Lord in our church," Ed Carter said one day during their visit. It had changed John's outlook on retirement. Maybe it wasn't about having more time for himself, but more time for God. John would love to put more time into his prayer ministry.

But did he have enough financial security to retire now, at fifty-five? Yes. John knew his stocks had done incredibly well, and truth be told, they could live reasonably well on Betty's pension alone.

Betty and John lived a simple life. They never paid much attention to the latest styles. They rarely went to movies. They much preferred their own cooking to that of restaurants. And, unlike his parents, neither of them had the urge to travel.

So, dear God in heaven, why not retire? It was time. He sensed that God had great things in mind for the prayer warrior John had become.

❧

"Are you sure you're an accountant?"

Rita couldn't help but laugh at his question. "I've been with the same CPA office since I graduated from UGA," she replied.

Ben smiled and shook his head. "I think of accountants as quiet people who only get excited about numbers."

Rita asked, "And are you sure you've been a dull old insurance underwriter your whole career?"

Ben Williams and Rita looked at each other, and then burst into laughter again. Never had two people chuckled and giggled and guffawed so much while looking at paintings in an art gallery. Who knew there was such hidden meaning in landscapes, portraits, and city scenes?

They'd seen pictures of buildings that had a resemblance to a famous rock singer and a car that, Ben could tell, had turned blue from holding its breath. Rita was sure that a cow serenely grazing in one picture was recovering from a wild night at the "sports barn." They both saw ridiculous accidents about to occur in the depiction of a royal coronation.

Now they looked through their Great Wall of China menus, trying to choose entrees from an incredible number of options.

Rita tried hard to focus on the task at hand, but her mind wandered to former dates with other men.

Most had taken her to movie houses, sporting events, bowling centers, or amusement parks; those places provided fun, in their very nature. Ben had taken her to a more sedate place, an art gallery, and made it fun by interacting with her.

Ben had a very caring nature. Other dates had opened car doors and restaurant doors for her; this guy opened them for anybody else too.

Rita suddenly realized a waiter was standing next to her, pencil and pad in hand. How long had he been waiting?

She blurted out, "I'll just have a cheeseburger and fries, please."

Ben convulsed with laughter. She realized what she'd done when the waiter said, "Sorry, Chinese restaurant no carry cheeseburger."

And she laughed, and the waiter laughed, too.

It wasn't jealousy, exactly. Arnold Miller, retired postmaster, had wanted to host a church service on his lawn ever since attending the one at Mary Eddy's a month ago.

He and Jolene immediately started planning where chairs, the speaker's stand, and the refreshment table would be.

"Brother Tom," Mr. Miller asked the pastor, "could Jolene and I host the next 'Church Inside Out' at our home?"

It was now the second Sunday night in November, and Ricky Temple had the impromptu congregation laughing about his old lifestyle.

"There are five basic directions," he continued. "Call them out after me as I point." The crowd was smiling, though many seemed a little unsure about what he meant.

Ricky pointed across the street. "North!" he proclaimed.

"North!" they responded.

"South," he called out, pointing in the opposite direction.

"South!" the crowd said.

"East," was his next indication.

"East!" they called back.

Ricky jumped to point in the opposite direction. "West!"

Immediately, "West!"

Ricky paused a moment, then quietly said, "And then, there was the direction I was going. Nowhere."

❧

Tom Osborn finally reached the phone on the seventh ring.

"Brother Tom? William Springstead. How are you?"

"Reverend Springstead! So good to hear from you," Tom said. "Life at Old Dominion is going really well. What can I do for you?"

William Springstead answered, "I'll be passing through Belton, Sunday after next. Thought I might stop in to visit."

"Reverend Springstead," Tom ventured, "I'd be honored if you would preach for us that Sunday. It would get our Advent season off to a great start."

Springstead answered, "Will do, young man. 'Always be ready to share the hope that is in you,' am I right?"

CHAPTER 39

Mandy Arthur had ceased to exist four years ago. The mother that loved Mandy had unexpectedly died four years ago, and her father had abandoned her to her grandparents. When she became Mandy Walton, legally adopted by Hank and Jeanette Walton, a new life began. Mandy thanked God for reaching down in mercy to not only save her but also give her a firm grounding in a loving home.

Ben picked up his guitar, sat on the padded stool, then winked at Mandy.

"This is going to be a blast!" Rita whispered, as she stepped to the microphone.

Rita scanned the Sunday morning congregation of Old Dominion United Methodist Church, and then began, "This is a song that Hank Walton wrote. Mandy and I have been singing it around the house for months, and we want to share it with you this morning. I want to thank Ben Williams for accompanying us on his guitar."

Rita stepped back, and Ben began strumming a simple tune. Mandy stepped up to her microphone.

> What am I doing, stumbling around?
> I'm walking so slow, with my eyes on the ground.

Worrying about things in a future so dim,
But it's not about me; it's all about him.

Rita and Ben joined in on the chorus:

It's not about me, and it's all about him,
Saving this world from its struggle with sin.
God reaches out to us all with his love.
It's not about me, and it's all about him.

We long for a life that's fulfilling and free,
But it can't be found in things centered on me,
Our eyes have to focus away from ourselves.
It's not about me, and it's all about him.

When they began the chorus again, people around the congregation were beginning to clap and sing along.

It's not about me, and it's all about him,
Saving this world from its struggle with sin.
God reaches out to us all with his love.
It's not about me, and it's all about him.

Two more verses followed. At the end, the congregation responded with enthusiastic applause. Rita gave Mandy a big hug as they returned to their regular pew and slipped her little hand into Ben's big one.

The thirty-something visitor in the Hawaiian shirt walked up after every other parishioner was gone. He clasped Tom's shoulder firmly and said, "I understand."

Tom said, "Excuse me?"

"I understand now why you can't decide about joining me at Collegetown," the visitor continued. "Man, this is the friendliest church I've ever been in! God's love is just oozing out of every crack. You've got everything here a pastor could want."

Tom finally figured it out.

"I'm humbled that you would take a Sunday morning to visit Old Dominion," Tom said. "Dale, it's nice to meet you in person. I want you to know that I have spent a lot of time in prayer about the position. I know God has had me in exactly the right place for the last year and a half."

"Look, Tom," Dale Rentz said, "you've really got it going here. I'd be surprised if you're not still here ten years from now. I just say, 'Go, God!' you know? Incredible worship today, man. 'Course, I'm more into contemporary music, but to each his own. Rock on, brother.

"But we'd be a great team for God in Collegetown. You've got organizational skills and people skills that I could only dream of. I'd be happy just to preach and write. Without an associate like you, our attendance will soon reach its limit. Think of all those people that would never be reached. Could you decide this week? I've got to get some help."

The Open Doors Sunday school class was always looking for ways to take their faith to the neighborhood near the church.

Last month's project was rejuvenating a nearby city park. The mayor's office gave permission for them to totally relandscape the park and to add two new pieces of playground equipment. The class also built and installed three new benches and created a quarter-mile walking track.

"Let's pray for our church's neighbors this month," Molly said.

"How will they know we're praying?" Ted asked.

Fran Smith shot out of her chair and said, "I know! I know! I know!" She was hopping up and down, practically bursting with excitement.

Laughter immediately erupted. "Fran," Erik said, "calm down a little and tell us your idea. Wow, this must be good!"

Fran stopped hopping, but she had to laugh at herself a little before she went on.

"Excuse me," she said. "I guess I got a little excited.

"What we should do," she continued, "is go out in teams of three and ask whoever comes to the door how we can pray for them. Then pray right there with them, right on their doorstep."

"That will be a great example of living inside out," Betty Lou Anderson said.

"And let's be sure to have a church leaflet to hand out," Keith Slappey said. "Wait! Better yet, let's make up one that has a place on it for prayer requests that they can mail back to us later."

"How about one," Molly asked, "that will hang on their doorknob, if they aren't home? Does anybody know how to make that?"

Maxine volunteered. "I made that kind of thing for work a year ago. I've still got it on my computer. Molly, you and I could work together on that."

"Sure," Molly said. "We could get together one night this week, and have some doorknob hangers ready for this Saturday. Who can go pray this Saturday?"

Sixteen hands were raised, amid various exuberant shouts.

"Woohoo!"

"Yeah, baby!"

"What an adventure!"

"We are AWESOME!"

"God is awesome-ER!"

CHAPTER 40

I t was ironic that less than half of the congregation had ever seen William Springstead before. His preaching on "inside out living" at last February's revival had propelled Old Dominion into its present surge in attendance and membership.

"Think I'm crazy, Keith?"

Tom Osborn waited for his building and grounds chairman to formulate an answer.

"Well, preacher," Keith Slappey replied, "I've only been at Old Dominion eight months, and I've never seen more than a hundred and twenty in here. Counting the choir, our church probably holds a hundred and forty. But you're our spiritual leader, and if you think we need more seating, Ricky, Ben, and I will make sure we set up enough folding chairs for at least a hundred and eighty."

Ricky chimed in. "This guy can really preach, Keith. People are going to turn out to hear him. Brother Springstead was the one that woke me up to the voice of Jesus."

"And then you changed enough to get me and Keith to notice, and we gave ourselves to Jesus," Ben added.

"I give William Springstead a lot of the credit for the church we've become," Tom said. "I'm looking forward to his being with us tomorrow."

Tom Osborn sat in his office on Saturday afternoon. What a year!

Since last February, forty people had joined Old Dominion. Some, like Keith Slappey, the Anderson family, Helen Adams, and Ricky Temple, had immediately thrown themselves wholeheartedly into the life of the church. Others were slowly but surely getting involved.

Long-time members had also made giant strides forward. John Carter ran a prayer ministry at his office now and was also teaching prayer classes at work and the church. After singing from the congregation for forty-two years, Beth Williams joined the choir. Betty Carter grew bushels of vegetables and gave almost all of them away as a means of reaching others for Christ. Rita Johnson regularly visited neighbors, near and far, to invite them to Christ and Old Dominion.

Susan Clark, owner of a local coffee shop, now closed the business on Sunday mornings to attend Old Dominion.

And then there was the elderly lady with the energy of a forty-year-old. Lydia Michaelson had stepped up to a higher level of generosity, using her money to inspire others to give more. Lydia recently committed two million dollars to the building of a new 250-seat sanctuary.

Tom knew that he also had been transformed by inside-out living. God was inspiring him with new ideas about outreach. Every visit to a gas station or a restaurant now was an adventure in faith sharing. The church had done two neighborhood outdoor worship services. Now Tom had asked the youth group to put together a Saturday night contemporary praise service.

As the pastor, Tom felt obliged to think ahead. Numbers were bothering him a little today. A new sanctuary was being planned, and it was already paid for. But would it be big enough?

He had set today as his deadline to call Dale Rentz. The offer was definitely attractive, even without the substantial pay raise. Tom's methods for church growth could be tested on a larger scale. He would have a secretary and other support staff.

Old Dominion would continue to grow without him, no doubt. Ricky Temple had really bought into the Biblical concept of encouraging one another, and would keep that ball rolling.

But Tom Osborn could continue to be very happy here.

Maybe the key factor was mileage. Between Collegetown and Helmsville.

"Who in the world are you people?" Reverend William Springstead said. He laughed heartily and continued. "Don't get me wrong, folks, I'm thrilled that you're here! But I was just here in February, and gracious, only a third of you were Old Dominionites then. Raise your hand if you've accepted Jesus as your Savior since the beginning of the year."

At least thirty persons out of one hundred seventy raised a hand. Exuberant applause broke out, with even a few whistles and hallelujahs.

"Wonderful! Wonderful!" Reverend Springstead said. "We are called to make disciples of all nations. Your pastor tells me that you are indeed about your Father's business.

"Do you love your fellow church members, as much as you love yourself?" he asked. Many heads nodded. A few even threw their arm around the person next to them.

"That can be a serious problem," William Springstead continued. He paused to let his words sink in. Many people looked confused.

"On this first Sunday in Advent, let's look at Matthew 1:18-25." Springstead proceeded to read the scripture, in a strong, animated style.

"Lord, open our eyes to the truth of your Word today. Amen."

Reverend Springstead stepped down from the pulpit and stood next to the communion table.

"Joseph was a righteous man, our Scripture says," Springstead continued. "He was a great church member. He followed the teaching of the synagogue. I am sure that he did his best to love his neighbor as himself, wouldn't you say?"

Many heads nodded, though some were noncommittal.

"Joseph, Mary's fiancé, was a righteous man. Yet God was asking him to do the wrong thing," Reverend Springstead said. "'Don't be afraid to marry the girl.' Choose God instead of your church friends; they would have had him put her away. And Joseph chose God, over what was right in the eyes of his church friends."

William Springstead wandered to the west windows.

"Brother Tom tells me that you will soon build a new sanctuary," he said. "Good people, soon after it is built, hopefully, you'll fill it up. If Old Dominion continues the same rate of growth, it won't take long. There's nothing wrong with that.

"But think about this: some of you are going to have to make a hard decision, to leave your friends in this service and start a second one. Or you will have to venture out to start another church. You love your friends here, but God calls you to continue reaching out to new people. Which will you choose: the comfort of old friends or the adventure of following God into the unknown?"

That question hit Tom Osborn right between the eyes.

Reverend William Springstead resumed his position at the podium.

"I am so proud of you," he said. "You've made a good start. But you *must keep* living inside out."

CHAPTER 41

"I hope you don't mind eating in a pub," said William Springstead. "Freddy's is famous around here for good food. And I'll bet it could use a few more Christians."

"No problem," responded Tom. "I've never been here before, but the food is great. Three of Old Dominion's finest young men are regulars here. One of them even led a Bible study here called "The High Life.""

The elder preacher laughed heartily. "That's quite an attention-getting name."

"It only lasted a few months, but I can't begin to tell you all the good it did."

"Well done. Tom, you've really hit the jackpot at Old Dominion. What a change in just a few months! It really glorifies God."

"So how will I know when to leave? I mean, the bishop makes a decision each year, and I vowed to serve where I'm sent. But how will I know when I should ask to move?"

"God will speak to you, son. When you are more valuable to him elsewhere, he'll make circumstances fall into place. You may be here ten more years, or this may be your last year."

Tom took a few more bites of his dessert.

"Tom, it was certainly an incredible service this morning, and I thank you for this envelope your treasurer handed me." Reverend Springstead retrieved an envelope from his pocket.

"A workman is worthy of his hire, the Bible says."

Reverend Springstead looked at the envelope, suddenly puzzled. He reached into another suit pocket, and seemed relieved to find another envelope.

"I'd forgotten, Tom, a lady gave me this envelope for you, when I was standing outside after church. It just says "Pastor Osborn" on the outside. I didn't know her.

After William Springstead left for his home, Tom settled into the chair in his office. He debated on whether to call Lawton Bradley immediately about the Sunnydale position, or to open the envelope. The envelope won.

"Call me.

You know I've been unhappy with my job at Calvary Baptist. I tried to work through it, knowing I should be happy to serve the Lord in any capacity. I still feel underappreciated, and now other staff members are grumbling about not getting a raise next year.

A couple weeks ago, I sent a resume to a church out of town, advertising for a Director of Children's Ministries. To my surprise, they responded positively. They have checked my references, and want to hire me after only a phone interview!

Call me! As soon as you can. Sylvia."

Tom's heartbeat wouldn't slow down. Would Sylvia leave him behind? Could they continue their romance at a distance?

Maybe he should propose to her, tonight. He'd been thinking about it for several days. That might just look like a desperate ploy to keep her from leaving.

If she left, why shouldn't he go to Collegetown? He could call Lawton right now.

He'd better call Sylvia first.

"Hi. It's Tom."

"I know, silly. My phone already told me."

"Sylvia, tell me about the job. This may be just what God has been preparing you for."

"Oh, Tom, I don't know what to do. The new church has a hundred kids, great facilities, and they think I'm just the one to take them to the next level. The pay would be double what I'm making now. And Janice Jenkins works there."

"Incredible. The Janice that was a good friend in seminary?"

"The very same. I think she may have put in a good word for me."

"I think you ought to take it."

"No! I can't! I don't want to be that far from you!"

"Where is it located?"

"It's at Orling United Methodist Church."

Tom began to laugh.

Sylvia cried, "What's wrong?"

He couldn't answer with anything but more laughter.

"What? What?!"

Tom managed to get control of himself. "Sylvia, did you know that the city of Orling is just five miles from Collegetown?"

"Well, I knew it was close. So what?"

"My dear, my love, I've been offered the associate pastor job at Sunnydale United Methodist Church. In Collegetown. Should I take it?"

"Great God in heaven! Awesome, awesome, awesome God! He reigns! He reigns!"

"Well?"

"Yes! And I'm going to Orling!"

Tom broke the news to a small group of friends first. They gathered for what they thought was a church planning session at Just What You Need on Monday night.

Tears flowed freely. In the end, Hank assured Tom they'd make him proud of Old Dominion. The inside-out movement would continue to drive the growth.

"Ricky," said Tom, "I name you the new Barnabas of Old Dominion United Methodist Church."

"What does that mean, exactly?" questioned Ricky.

"Barnabas means 'son of encouragement.'"

"I'll serve with gladness. Who do you think they'll name as our interim pastor until the new appointments in June?"

Tom flashed his customary grin. "I just heard this afternoon. It's a seasoned pastor who retired too early, by the name of William Springstead."

Two hundred people gathered in the sanctuary of Old Dominion on the Sunday night between Christmas and New Years, to say goodbye to their beloved pastor. No previous pastor had presided over the incredible growth Tom Osborn had, though his year-and-a-half tenure was also the shortest in this church's history.

After eight different speakers had praised Tom's various abilities and accomplishments, the pastor was given the opportunity to speak.

"To God be the glory. I've made very dear friends here during my short stay, and I'll miss you terribly. I even had the privilege of leading many of you to the Lord, for which I can't thank God enough. You've taught me so much. The kind of pastor I was when I arrived here could not have led you to the place you are today. Again, to God be the glory.

"I learned to put most of my energy into encouraging you to think of others first. We call that living inside out. That's why our little church has experienced such growth. You've done the living, I've done the encouraging, all of us led and empowered by God.

"I guess you've heard that I'm not the only one starting a new job on January first. Sylvia, come on up to the front so that people can see you."

Sylvia Beattie made her way to the platform at the front of the church, as Tom continued.

"Sylvia Beattie and I were in seminary together, then lost track of each other until last year. She has been the Children's Minister at Calvary Baptist Church, near Helmsville. She has taken the position of Director of Children's Ministries at Orling United Methodist Church, which is only five miles from where I'll be serving in Collegetown."

The congregation applauded Sylvia's good news and Tom's blessing of having her nearby.

He continued, "Sylvia has become very important to me in the past year. Very important. And I'm going to give her a chance to say a word after I ask a very important question."

As the congregation listened intently for Tom's question, he slipped his hand into his pocket and pulled out a small box. Looking at Sylvia, he dropped to one knee and asked, "Sylvia Beattie, will you marry me?"

Sylvia made the shortest speech of the night: "Yes!"